"Visiting Joplin after the [...] hand the devastating destruction Mother Nature wrought on this community, but also the strength of spirit in the citizens of Joplin. City Manager, Mark Rohr's book, *Joplin: The Miracle of the Human Spirit* vividly recounts the quick thinking, the recovery process, and plan of rebuilding that was necessary to secure Joplin's future. After reading Mark's book it will become clear why Missouri embodies the "Heartland" of our nation, where you always help a neighbor in need and value family, friends, church, and hard work."

—Kit Bond, United States Senator; Missouri

"Though Mark and I have talked many times about the events surrounding the tornado of May 22nd, 2011, his book brings back those chaotic hours and days as if it happened yesterday. I'm anxious for others to read *Joplin: The Miracle of the Human Spirit;* they will learn about the multitude of heroic acts that unfolded in our community."

—Mike Woolston, Mayor
Joplin, Missouri

"I live about 60 miles from Joplin, and I was stunned to see the huge path of destruction in the days after this incredible disaster. Moments after the tornado hit, state and local officials had to make decisions that would impact the region's future for generations to come. Missourians are resilient, and as always, neighbors served as both the first and the last responders during this critical time of need. Today, the area is alive with new businesses, new homes, and the welcome signs of continued recovery. I'm very grateful for the dedicated state and local officials—along with countless volunteers from all over America—who came together to help the people of Joplin."

—U.S. Senator Roy Blunt, Missouri

JOPLIN

THE MIRACLE
OF THE
HUMAN SPIRIT

JOPLIN

THE MIRACLE OF THE HUMAN SPIRIT

BY JOPLIN CITY MANAGER

MARK ROHR

TATE PUBLISHING
AND ENTERPRISES, LLC

Published by Tate Publishing & Enterprises, LLC
127 E. Trade Center Terrace | Mustang, Oklahoma 73064 USA
1.888.361.9473 | www.tatepublishing.com

Tate Publishing is committed to excellence in the publishing industry. The company reflects the philosophy established by the founders, based on Psalm 68:11,
"The Lord gave the word and great was the company of those who published it."

Book design copyright © 2012 by Tate Publishing, LLC. All rights reserved.
Cover design by Leah LeFlore
Interior design by Nathan Harmony
Photos courtesy of Pat Nagel

Published in the United States of America

ISBN: 978-1-62024-703-7
1. Biography & Autobiography / Personal Memoirs
2. History / United States / State & Local / Midwest
12.04.17

Dedication

This book is dedicated to the 161 Victims of the May 22nd, 2011 Joplin Tornado. They will live on in our hearts and their spirits will inspire generations to come.

Table of Contents

Introduction

We know about tornados. Here in the Midwest, we know spring's arrival brings weather alerts you should take seriously. There's always that eerie calm before the storm that turns eyes upward as clouds begin to swirl, mixing cold and tepid air, about to spawn nature's worst. When the tornado siren sounds, we take cover. We have learned to heed the ominous warnings because we have seen and felt the effects of monster whirlwinds descending from darkened skies, then steamrolling across the land, literally ripping to shreds anything in its path. On May 22nd, 2011, our neighbors in Joplin, Missouri experienced the fury of EF-5 winds that left a third of their city in shambles and took the lives of 161 people. They, too, know about tornados, but nothing prepared them for this kind of devastation; this kind of loss.

Mark Rohr, Joplin's City Manager, found himself personally thrust into dealing with the aftermath of the storm as he helped free victims from the remains of a flattened church near the storm's epicenter. He and other first responders would spend hours on end, digging through debris—what was left of homes, businesses, schools, and lives.

Joplin: The Miracle of the Human Spirit is an important book for two major reasons:

It is the story of how a community rallies to fight for survival against all odds and how caring outsiders felt their pain

11

and came to help by the thousands. The citizens of Joplin never gave up or gave in. They were determined to see their city restored in appearance as well as spirit.

The book also gives us insight into the responsibilities of city government during such disaster. The book is a record of Mark's responsibilities, decisions and events during the first six months following the storm; events that would change Joplin forever. There was no manual, no clear direction as to how to respond to such overwhelming needs, so Mark Rohr and his staff began to write the book on disaster response. Based on a daily journal Mark kept from the beginning, the book gives the reader a behind the scenes glimpse into the priorities, the meetings, the proposals, the details, the inner workings of an organized plan to bring Joplin back even better than before. Implementing his 10 Tenets of Disaster Response, Mark created a blueprint to benefit other communities facing similar situations.

We are honored to publish "Joplin: The Miracle of the Human Spirit." There is an old story of a seaman who said, "In fierce storms, we must do one thing; there is only one way; we must put the ship in a certain position and keep her there." Mark Rohr, and dedicated leaders like him, put Joplin on a course and held her there during the aftermath of the storm, giving her the greatest opportunity to heal and one day rise again.

If you happen to be traveling down Interstate 144, turn off and head north to spend some time in a great American city…witness "The Miracle of the Human Spirit" for yourself. It's alive and well in Joplin!

—Ryan Tate, President and CEO
Tate Publishing & Enterprises

A Third of Joplin in Ruins

"Forty five seconds and it was over. 45 long seconds. We looked at each other, terrified, and thanked God we were alive."

—Dr. Kevin Kitka, Emergency Physician
St. John's Regional Medical Center, Joplin

I have always felt that my entire life had been a preparation for a great challenge. I had known other challenges, the hardest of which was dealing with my mother's death when I was sixteen years old. Some of the challenges I tackled in my career as City Manager for previous posts were not simple fixes either. I had found myself serving cities which needed to be rebuilt or revitalized. Part of my professional agenda was to find ways to infuse those cities with new life or vision; to develop an aggressive effort toward improvement and growth. I had no way of knowing on the morning of May 22, 2011, how grateful I would be for this level of experience. I would come to depend on it greatly by day's end.

On May 22nd, 2011, at 5:50 p.m., I received a call informing me of what would turn out to be, the greatest challenge of my career. The call was from Joplin's Fire Chief, Mitch Randles, relaying to me that the city I manage, Joplin, Missouri had just been hit by a devastating tornado. I had been the City Manger for Joplin since November of 2004.

I was not aware then, that this would prove to be the deadliest tornado in the United States, since the National Weather Service began keeping official records in 1950. Effectively, one-third of Joplin had been removed from the map.

Cubs vs. the Red Sox on ESPN

That Sunday morning of May 22nd was like most spring mornings in the Midwest. It was cool, but most likely to warm up considerably by the afternoon. I had been home on the south end of the city, enjoying the day off, unaware of any threatening weather. In fact, I was finishing up some last minute chores, preparing to watch some television. The Cubs were to play the Red Sox that evening at Fenway Park on ESPN's Sunday Night Baseball. Walking around the house attending to those tasks, I was not able to answer Mitch's call right away, although I had heard my phone ring. When I could, I dropped what I was doing and played the message he left.

"Mark a good part of the city has been hit by a huge tornado—it's bad! Call as soon as possible."

His voice was remarkably calm, given what he was dealing with during those first moments of the storm's aftermath. I called him back immediately. He gave me all the details he knew at that time. The storm had left devastation like he'd never seen. He said he was assisting people at El Vaquero's, a Mexican restaurant on Main Street. Suddenly, the baseball game was of little relevance.

My wife was returning from Springfield, Missouri sixty miles away where she had picked up my stepson, Miles, age 11, after a weekend visit with his father. Our two children, four year old Ryan, and Riley, two years old, were also in the car with her. As I found my shoes and windbreaker, I called Lois with a frantic message to get off the highway and take cover in the nearest building, since I knew she was heading in our direction. She called back just as I was leaving the house and I reiterated the message.

"Lois, get off the highway and find a safe place for you and the kids to wait out this storm. I've got to go, please be safe."

Unprepared for What I Saw

I left our house in the southern part of Joplin, just a block off Main, driving north to meet up with the fire chief, unprepared for what I would find. Wearing the clothes I would be in for the next 30 hours, I drove north on Main Street toward the restaurant Mitch had mentioned. As I crossed 32nd street, I began to see on the horizon the effects of what this tornado had done to our town. The further north I drove on Main Street, the worse the view became and it was difficult to take it all in: debris everywhere, fallen trees, missing buildings and homes. I knew I needed to find Mitch as soon as possible.

Along the way, I saw downed power lines covering the road. I looked to see if there were sparks which would indicate the lines were live. They didn't appear to be, so I decided to drive over them to get to my destination. Nothing looked familiar. It was hard to tell exactly where I was at times, because street signs were gone and the whole area looked like a bomb had been dropped, leveling everything in sight.

Finally, with too much blockage in the roadway, I parked my SUV in the parking lot of the former J-Town bar, which had recently been converted into a Salvation Army thrift store. I ran the remaining two blocks to meet up with Mitch, who was helping in the rescue of citizens trapped in the storm's rubble. I was in utter disbelief of the total chaos and devastation.

I saw Mitch standing near the remains of the restaurant. I stopped to survey the scope of damage in the parking lot and the surrounding area. It elicited thoughts of the worst apocalyptic movies I had ever seen. My review of the damage stopped when I spotted a minivan about ten feet away. The windshield of the vehicle had been blown out and the occupants, two men were sitting upright, both vacantly looking forward, as if caught by surprise. Unfortunately, these two deceased individuals were part of the grim statistics of the storm: the monster tornado would claim 161 lives.

Like others, I saw many sights that night I'm sure I will never see again in my life time. Some, I cannot erase from my mind, although I have tried. Others, I hope I never forget. I said a silent prayer for the anonymous victims in front of me and tried to compose myself. I knew that some things, for me and many others, would never be the same; things like perspective on life and death, priorities, human endurance and loss. My role as City Manager now required me to take action on a much larger scale than ever before. And time was of the essence because lives were on the line. I had to act quickly.

First Actions Amid the Chaos

I ran to a Joplin police officer standing nearby and asked him to contact the 911 Communications Center, via the radio in his car, to have them call out all of my department heads to meet immediately at the Emergency Operations Center (EOC) in the basement of the Safety Center. The Donald E. Clark Safety Center, at 303 E. 3rd Street housed both the Joplin Police Department and Joplin Fire Department. I had no idea at that point that the Center, in specific the basement of the building, would be my home for the next four weeks.

After making sure the call was made, I turned to Mitch, "We have to assess the extent of the damage, because, if it is this bad here, I need to find out about the damage to the rest of the town."

Luckily, I knew from previous weather events that assessing damage was the initial crucial step in a city's response to a storm or disaster. I was City Manager of Washington Courthouse, Ohio, in the early 1990's, when straight-line winds moved through that city causing damage. It was a mess for a while, but nothing in comparison to what the Joplin tornado left in its wake.

Mitch and I jumped into his SUV and headed north on Main Street. What we saw was so surreal that neither one of us spoke for a time. We passed through this older, established area of town, where once there had been well kept businesses and offices on the tree lined street. Every building was severely damaged or completely gone. People were climbing out from the rubble, dazed, crying; smoke and dust was everywhere. Others were staggering down the debris-filled roads, eyes wide with shock and fear. An acrid smell permeated the air.

I had experienced the eerie calm that usually follows a storm, but this was different. The twister expelled its rage, and then simply moved on; leaving behind such a thick atmosphere you could almost touch it.

Mitch turned onto 20th Street, following his well-honed emergency instincts. This east-west road was a major thoroughfare in Joplin that fronted the local high school, the vocational school, a grocery store, and several apartment complexes.

We had traveled eastward well over a quarter of a mile on 20th street when Mitch pointed out to our right that the vocational school was completely leveled. The nearby high school, Joplin High School, built in the 1950's, had not fared much better with approximately one-half of the brick structure building caved in. Mercifully, the tornado struck on a Sunday and school had not been in session. My mind raced to the consequences had this been a weekday. Continuing east, we crossed the railroad tracks, where a lady frantically waved us down.

"There's a church to the north of 20th Street. It has collapsed and there are people trapped inside!" she shouted.

Where's the Church—Gone!

Mitch pulled the vehicle down the street leading to the heap of destruction which moments before had been the Joplin Full Gospel Church at 20th and Michigan. We both hurriedly exited the SUV. I continued to be impressed with the calmness and professionalism with which Mitch was handling the situation.

The small church building had been flattened, only rubble remained. As usual on Sunday evenings, the church was conducting services with several people in attendance. There was a group of five to ten people trying to move the pieces of building remnants to access the people trapped in the debris. I could hear children screaming and others crying underneath the destroyed structure. There was so much to take in that I continually had to remind myself: *Focus, Mark; these folks need your help.*

We moved to the northernmost section where the majority of activity was taking place. Some of the men on the site told us a lady with a severed leg was in the bed of a pickup truck awaiting transportation to the hospital. We joined others and continued to work furiously to remove the huge chunks of wood, bricks, sheetrock, and twisted metal.

Twenty minutes prior I had been planning to watch a baseball game and relax for the evening. Now, I was thrust into a battle against time to save lives. I will never forget the screams from women and children calling for help underneath the obliterated structure. We were reaching them slowly but surely; some were injured, some deceased, and some survived without a scratch.

Mitch moved to the northeasterly portion of the toppled church and quickly started helping others free victims there. I remained to the east and helped a team of men who were lifting wood and aluminum from the pile. As I stood on this pile, I remember thinking, *Oh God, I hope no one is lying beneath where I'm standing.*

I looked over at Mitch who was working to my left. Beside him on the ground, about ten feet away from the structure, was a beautiful young girl who appeared to be only six or seven years old. She was clearly deceased. As she lay on the grass, no one had time to mourn her passing, though tragic; everyone was frantically working around her to help the others trapped alive.

Glancing at the young girl's lifeless body, I felt a wave of nausea as I thought of my own beautiful two year old daughter, Riley, whom I hoped had made it through the storm along with the rest of my family. We found another young girl alive under the piles of building materials. She was crying as she was lifted from the debris, but her facial expression told us she was relieved to see daylight.

A middle-aged lady was rescued similarly. Behind her was yet another lady that appeared to have suffered a broken leg. I worked with two other men to gently move her to the side so we could get to other people. She was hysterical, screaming out a name, which I assumed was the name of her child. She asked the pastor about her loved one. This caring clergyman, in an incredibly difficult situation, told her that her loved one was fine, but I was fearful that was not the case. Later, I would spend many days in the EOC monitoring information which included the names of the deceased. In this instance, I wish I had been wrong about the well-being of the dear lady's loved one. The name she was calling for turned out to be her husband and not her child. His name was on the death list.

One More Victim

Continuing our efforts to move the massive amount of debris that was the remains of the church in order to find any other survivors, we uncovered a lady that appeared to be dead. Her head was resting next to me and her feet closest to the two rescuers I was helping. The two men at her feet agreed that she was deceased and needed to be moved so we could reach others.

"Lift her under the arms and we will grab the feet," someone directed.

This was the closest I had ever been to someone that had passed away. I gathered myself, took a deep breath and lifted her upper body while the others lifted her feet. We carried her ten feet or so toward an open area and gently laid her on the ground. Once we moved her, we were able to find more trapped individuals and pull them free. Again, my thoughts returned to my wife, children and step-children. I prayed silently, *God, I don't know where my family is, or if they have escaped this horrible calamity. Please take care of them while I work to help these people.*

A Plan in the Making

After about thirty minutes, it appeared as though the scene at the church had been stabilized enough that Mitch and I felt comfortable to leave. We needed to get to the EOC to assess the extent of the storm damage and to develop a plan to respond to the situation for the entire city. I knew that in my capacity as City Manager, I would have to be the person responsible for developing a widespread response plan. While witnessing the hundreds of citizens of Joplin rallying to help their fellow citizens, I felt I could do the most good by working with my department heads and fellow city employees in activating a plan to respond to the storm's fierce impact.

To the best of my knowledge, we arrived back at the EOC at approximately 6:30 p.m., about an hour after the tornado tore through Joplin. My recollection of the next three hours is murky at best. I had just left a horrific scene, and, in reflection, can't help but think that the lack of my specific recall over the next three hours was my mind's way of protecting itself. I didn't have time to deal with or process completely the pain and loss I witnessed at the church site that evening? I tried to focus on the need to take appropriate action for Joplin's future. However, I'm sure I was a little dazed by all I had seen and heard during those first few minutes.

What I do recall of that evening was directing Police Chief, Lane Roberts, to assign two of his best employees to immediately begin to survey the damage to the city. I would need their report to know what resources we had available locally and what help we would need to request from other sources. Based on the similar experience mentioned earlier, when I served Washington Courthouse, Ohio in the early 90's, I knew I had to get organized.

I then instructed the Assistant City Manager, Sam Anselm, to start contacting cities all over the region and state requesting help. I knew that we would need more boots on the ground than Joplin alone could muster. We couldn't afford to wait for the police department assessment to request the help. Poor Sam had only been with the city for six weeks by May 22nd. He had come from a similar position in a small city outside of St. Louis, Missouri and his learning curve had been accelerated greatly in the last few moments. Sam did an excellent job of rising to the occasion.

I also remember calling my wife, Lois, a dozen or more times, to no avail. I needed to focus on the enormous task at hand, but was desperate to hear if she and all five children were safe. I learned later that cell phone service for most of the Joplin area was non-existent, as towers enabling the service had been knocked out of service. I asked my administrative assistant, Vicki Coots, to continue to call Lois' phone while Mitch and I prepared to board a helicopter supplied by a Tulsa hospital to view by air the damage wreaked by the storm.

By that time, the EOC was a flurry of activity. The Emergency Operation Center was coming together as designed, staffed by the necessary people to make it work. This post would be the central point for operating the city's plan to respond to the storm's damage. I was anxiously awaiting the police's damage assessment report. It was now around 9:30 p.m. and the officers had been dispatched around 6:30, so, I wondered what was taking them so long.

The helicopter had landed in the city parking lot to the south of The Safety Center, used primarily as parking for the city's Municipal Court. After receiving instructions on the communication devices affixed to the protective helmet and the drop down night-vision goggles, we boarded the helicopter. As I watched litter churn in the parking lot from the wash of the propellers, I looked at the time on my useless phone. My thoughts turned again to my family. I still didn't know if they were safe. As we lifted off, I prayed again for their safety and well being.

By now, Fire Chief Mitch Randles had received news that his house in neighboring Duquesne, a small community just east of Joplin, had been destroyed. On a side note, Mitch and his family had been heading home on the afternoon of May 22nd, following his son's high school graduation. When the first storm warnings began to come in, something or *Someone* urged him to change the plan. Instead of returning home, Mitch took his family to the Fire Station to wait out the storm. Call it a hunch or simple fate, but, I call it divine intervention that caused Mitch to heed the warnings about the seriousness of the storm. If they had returned home the family certainly would have been in harm's way. Mitch asked the helicopter pilot to take us over Duquesne to see the area where his home stood; it was completely demolished. Even while viewing the site from the air, Mitch remained amazingly focused on task.

Once we lifted off for the helicopter tour, it did not take long to realize why the damage assessment team from the police department had not returned with their report yet.

We started on the west end of the city and followed the path of the storm easterly. I was shocked by what I saw. The storm had cut a swath of devastation from 1/2 mile to 3/4 of a mile wide, extending for six miles across the city from the western boundary to our eastern boundary and beyond. From what we could see, very little was left in the tornado's wake. A third of the town of 50,000 inhabitants had been impacted.

Thank God, Family is Okay

Months later, reporters would ask, "What was your response after first seeing the damage from the air?" I responded honestly, "I feel overwhelmed by the task at hand." The level of destruction defied description. But, I knew I would only have the luxury of being overwhelmed for about fifteen seconds and that if I harbored that feeling for too long, what hope did the citizens of Joplin have? I had to find out about my family, assess the damage, and then get to work...in that order.

When I returned to the basement of the Safety Center, I was hugely relieved to hear that Lois had been able to text a brief message of "OK" to my administrative assistant. I took the response to mean she and the kids were fine. I wanted to know what had happened to them, but knowing my family was safe, gave me added focus on developing a response plan for Joplin.

I later learned that my oldest stepson, Michael, 17, who was also driving back with his cousin from the high school graduation program, outran the storm and made it safely to his uncle's home in Joplin, outside the tornado area, before the storm made the city. Step-daughter, Meagan, 19, had been working at the Lowe's on Rangeline Road and was safe as well. Then, as stated, 11 year old stepson, Miles, and our two young ones, Riley and Ryan, had been with Lois. All were safe and sound. *Thank you, God.*

I have thought back many times on those first few hours after Mitch's call. Statistics would show later how many homes and business were destroyed on May 22nd, 2011. There would also be the report of how many folks were injured and how many Joplin residents lost their lives that day. But the acts of courage and real heroism, the stories of determination and perseverance, the attitude and dedication of Joplin's public servants—those stories would not be included in cold statistics, yet they were just beginning to be told. Over the next days and months I would be in awe of the everyday heroes who live among us. They were there from the very beginning.

Making it Up As We Go

"That was just the way my son was. That was Chris. I'm glad he saved those lives…As a mom, you're proud, but it doesn't bring him back. That's my conflict."

—Pamela Praytor, mother of
Christopher Lucas, 27
Chris lost his life on May 22, 2012,
after making sure customers
and fellow employees were safe

There was no instruction book available to us in the aftermath of the EF-5 tornado that devastated Joplin on May 22, 2011. Most cities have an Emergency Operations Manual, which, in my experience, usually consists of little more than a contacts list. I'm pretty sure the officials that draft such documents never envisioned a catastrophe of the magnitude we were facing. By sheer necessity, we would have to make up our response as we went.

From the age of five, I grew up in Cincinnati, Ohio, one of three children. I was the middle child, with an older sister and younger sister. I made good grades and participated in sports, even though I was smaller than my classmates, due to my late

December birthday. In my earliest memories, I was the one to organize neighborhood teams, plan the adventures, and come up with a way to entertain ourselves. My sisters would always say, that I could "plan the fun out of any activity." I suppose that was because I had a strong need for structure and organization which demonstrated itself even in childhood. After graduating with a Masters in Public Administration from Xavier University in 1984 I served as City Manager to four cities. In 2004, I became City Manager for Joplin, Missouri with an operating budget of $147,000,000 a year and 650 city employees. During those first challenging hours after the tornado of May 22, 2011, I would be grateful for my tendencies toward organization and the previous experiences that would serve me well throughout the coming ordeal.

No Finer Team

I will always be grateful for a core group of fifteen professional department heads that I could rely upon. They, too, were willing to help "make it up as we went." They would surround me with support as we worked through that Sunday night and for weeks to come. I would utilize their various areas of expertise as the need for each arose, at the appropriate time, and as we approached the different stages of our response.

First Things First—Search and Rescue

The initial, immediate concerns were for the safety and well-being of our citizens and as such we directed our initial efforts to the search and rescue aspect of disaster response. Just moments following the storm, citizens themselves became the first responders as they began to dig through the rubble left by the monster twister to locate family members, friends, and neighbors. A more organized search would be implemented on the next day. At this time, we had no way of knowing how many lives had been lost.

Finally, I received word through the police chief, Lane Roberts, regarding the report from those assigned officers who had been charged with accessing damage. Their report confirmed the widespread level of destruction, giving me further perspective on what I had seen earlier through the night vision goggles aboard the chopper.

Our immediate goal was paramount: to rescue anyone still trapped in the rubble. We had enlisted the help of many police and fire departments who were on their way to help. Mainly, the help would come from the surrounding four state regions of Missouri, Oklahoma, Arkansas, and Kansas. In addition, there were hundreds of ordinary folks who heard about the tornado and jumped into their cars and made the trip to Joplin to volunteer their help. There were entire families arriving to help us.

Police Chief, Roberts, and Fire Chief, Mitch Randles, both very capable professionals, were working with their staffs to organize the deployment of this help. I can recall telling them that at least one person from our departments needs to accompany these safety forces as most would not be familiar with our city. The Fire Department had already been at work dividing Joplin into grids to coordinate rescue efforts. Teams of volunteers would be assigned each particular grid or portion of the city affected, until all were thoroughly searched.

My assistant, Sam, had been busy making contact with surrounding cities for assistance. We had legions of public works employees, mostly made up of road crews, arriving to assist our local crews, plus those of the Missouri Department of Transportation to clear the streets. Their task was to clear the roadway (both sides of every street) before emergency vehicles could get into the areas most impacted. We would hear later, from those who were in the disaster response business, this was done in record time and proved to be instrumental in setting the stage for other response successes to follow. FEMA officials praised these efforts and were surprised at the progress made even before they arrived in Joplin.

Utilizing the information from the police department, combined with what Mitch Rundles and I had seen in our overhead view, we were now able to put together a map of the damage. It appeared as though the storm damaged an area six miles in length and 3/4 of a mile wide from the city's western border to its eastern border.

Dealing With Nationwide Media Interest

As our plans were developing, we realized that the national media would be descending on us at daybreak on May 23rd, the second day of dealing with the disaster. With that thought in mind and the need to allay the concerns of Joplin's citizens, Joplin's Public Information Officer, Lynn Onstot, and I scheduled a press conference to be held in the parking lot of Cunningham Park at 5:30 a.m. Cunningham Park, the oldest park in the city, located at the corner of Maiden Lane and 26th Street, had been in the storm's path and was totally destroyed. The park sat directly across from St. John's Regional Medical Hospital, a nine story structure also significantly damaged by the tornado. We would learn later that the storm had intensified in strength just as it approached the area in which St. John's and Cunningham Park are located.

Working with Lynn, who had worked in Joplin for many years, we prepared a written statement thinking a structured statement was the best approach in an unstructured environment. The statement would include that there had been 89 confirmed deaths at that point. Here below is that first statement issued on the morning of May 23rd, unedited—just as it was delivered:

> The city of Joplin suffered a tragedy and our hearts go out to all affected in this disaster. At approximately 5:45 p.m., Sunday, May 22nd, a tornado started on the western city limits and traveled through the middle of our city. This tornado tore a destructive path starting at the 28th and Schifferdecker area and moved eastward for approximately 6 miles. The path was at least 1/2 mile wide and possibly larger in some areas. This tornado went through a major residential part of our city, and damaged a large commercial district in the Rangeline area before it moved out of Joplin. Many homes and buildings have suffered extensive damage, with many being a total loss.
>
> We know many people are hurting at this time. It is a sad day in Joplin. It is with a sad heart I report that we have 89 confirmed deaths due to this tornado. The city's priority is to take care of the victims by completing a thorough search and rescue effort in cooperation with many of the area's emergency medical service personnel. We have continued this through the night and anticipate that this effort will be ongoing for the next few days.

Other cities and communities have stepped forward to help Joplin during our time of distress. We have approximately over 40 agencies helping with our public safety issues, as well as infrastructure needs. Many public works crews have traveled to Joplin to provide assistance with road clearance, and major needs. There are approximately 410 personnel members involved in this effort. We have declared a local emergency and the state of emergency due to this tornado and its destruction. We have seen homes impacted, as well as schools, churches, businesses and one of our hospitals, which we are standing near that area. We are working closely also with our utility partners in Joplin, as well as the school district and medical organizations. All have been affected, but we are pulling together in our Emergency Operation Center to ensure that our citizens are safe and informed as we go through this tragedy. We continue to ask our residents for their patience during this time. We will recover and come back stronger than we are today. Thank you.

I knew Joplin was getting national media attention due to the storm, but, I was surprised to see the number of news vans, television crews and reporters at the park site at such an early hour. The message I delivered that day was designed to provide information and demonstrate that the city was in control of the situation. I wanted to be clear that Joplin was not only emotionally moved by the extent of the disaster, but we were also implementing a plan in response to the critical circumstances.

Following the early morning press conference, several city officials including Mayor Mike Woolston, Fire Chief Mitch

Randles, and myself were asked to appear live on the major morning news shows. I had walked across 26th Street, onto St. John's hospital property for my interview with CBS. As we were preparing to go live on camera, I looked down at a nearby pile of rubble and spotted a baby's Nike tennis shoe. I found myself suddenly fighting back tears while I stood surrounded by indescribable destruction and debris. I uttered a silent prayer, *"Please God, may the owner of that little shoe be alive."* I composed myself just in time to respond to the interviewer's first question.

For the most part, dealings with the media throughout the entire event have been very positive. We received fair and honest coverage and the questions reporters raised were of genuine interest to the public. The army of press people descending on Joplin, especially during those first days, not only informed the world of the tragedy, but, also helped to send the message that Joplin needed the help and prayers of our nation.

Searching Through the Debris Was Priority One

We traveled back to the EOC to begin a series of meetings, which in retrospect, and perhaps due to lack of sleep, remain a little foggy in my mind. I recall a significant number of elected officials convening in the basement of the Donald E. Clark Safety Center. They had good intentions and wanted to help, but until we had our basic plan fully operational there was little else anyone could suggest.

Overnight, the Fire Department had developed a search and rescue plan for the storm-damaged area. Our first order of business was to search for people who could still be trapped in the rubble. We had a lot of debris to search through. That is an understatement. We didn't know specific numbers then, but it would later be determined that an estimated 3 million cubic yards of debris was left by the tornado. To put this in perspective, one million cubic yards of debris would fill the interior of Kansas City's Arrowhead Stadium then continue beyond to a height of 510 feet above its rim. So imagine the amount of debris it would take to more than triple that amount and more.

It was still early in the morning when safety personnel from all over the state and region filled the bays of the Joplin Fire Department's main station. Although I didn't count, there had to be at least 500 volunteers reporting for duty. The plan, delivered by our Fire Department Management Team, called for utilizing their assistance by dividing them into teams to comb the storm area. Our crews and citizens themselves, who had maintained an all-night search, were about to get some much needed help.

Although, we would all play multiple roles for the immediate and foreseeable future, the Joplin Police Department aided by the National Guard from the state of Missouri would focus on directing traffic and maintaining a semblance of order in the extremely chaotic environment.

Public works' crews from all over had been summoned, by my assistant's calls for aid. They would arrive at various intervals during the day following the storm and report to the Public Works Center on 4th Street, about a mile west of the Safety Center. I had tasked them with clearing the streets of debris, which as stated, was crucial to the search and rescue effort.

Determining the Storm's Strength

Later, on the same morning, officials from the National Weather Service had arrived on scene and wanted to talk with me and Mitch, the fire chief. By that time, the core EOC room was swelling with occupants, so we met with these officials in an adjoining room. We had been up all night and were starting to show the evidence of fatigue.

Following introductions, one of the experts, a younger man, proceeded to tell us he thought the tornado was in the EF3 category. Tornados are measured in terms of wind speed on the Enhanced Fujita scale. An EF3 tornado means the wind speed reached 136 to 165 miles per hour. If a tornado is designated as EF4, the wind speed is from 166 to 200 miles per hour. A category EF5 tornado means wind speeds exceed 200 miles per hour. I appreciate weather professionals and their expertise, but, when it was suggested the tornado that hit Joplin was only an EF3, Mitch and I looked at each other and we were both thinking: *Like hell it was an EF3!*

We had both observed the level of destruction brought on by this storm and knew intuitively this first estimate was off the mark. Neither one of us said anything in response, but we must have looked stunned. When the young man left the room, an older professional with the Weather service stated the storm was, in his opinion, at least an EF4. Mitch and I nodded in agreement.

While huddled in a small room at the local Armory, we encountered these same two gentlemen later the same day. At that point, the younger man who had suggested the EF3 category, said,

"I now believe it was an EF4, with wind speeds up to 198 miles per hour."

I thought to myself, *198 but not 200? How can he possibly calculate such a slight difference?* He said assigning a higher EF5 designation would be a "political decision!" In essence, he was saying, this would be the call of those "higher up" at the National Weather Service. I thought the reference to any type of politics seemed absurd at that moment. We would learn in the subsequent days that whether "politics" were applied, or not, the National Weather Service designated the Joplin tornado as an EF5. The winds that tore through Joplin on May 22nd, 2011 were in excess of 200 miles per hour.

Setting Up Offices to Work From

Once we had crews working in the field, we settled into our respective work areas at the EOC. I claimed the space adjoining the main EOC room, where we had earlier met with the National Weather Service representatives. Only bare necessities were placed in the makeshift offices. My computer sat on a counter top. I grabbed a couple of folding chairs to be used by those coming in and out constantly. I would use this same space for meeting with department heads, also.

In the main EOC room, fire department personnel had established a post along the eastern wall of the basement. Reports from crews working in the field regarding search efforts would be received here by radio. We were pleased with early reports of rescues that were taking place, but that short term euphoria was over overshadowed by the grim death count tally. Those numbers were growing.

The Public's Need to Know

Joplin Public Information Officer, Lynn Onstot, reminded me of the growing national attention Joplin was receiving and suggested another press conference for mid-afternoon of Monday, May 23rd. We decided to conduct all press conferences in the parking lot of Cunningham Park, where we held our press briefing at 5:30 a.m. that morning. We thought the setting was helpful to convey information, challenges we were encountering, along with reports of progress. The images of the destruction in the background, gave the rest of the country some idea of the severity of the storm. It helped tell the story.

I was quickly learning how challenging these press conferences would be. Information would flow in from various city staff up to the time set for the briefing to begin. I was not comfortable just "winging" it, so I always read a prepared statement, followed by an opportunity for the reporters to ask questions. I would soon discover that these meetings with the media would be like cramming for finals in college in some instances. I would outline what I wanted to include in the press reports, but then tried to reiterate to department heads how important it was to have the most accurate, up to date information available. Often, I would not receive the data until just before the scheduled conference without even having an opportunity to read over the reports.

Of course, also during the first press conferences on Monday following the disaster, I had to appear professional and lucid after being up all night. I was continually aware, that my words would impact lives—not only what I said, but how it was said would be important. The information I shared would shape the perception of others and how the world viewed our city as we experienced this catastrophe.

The Governor Arrives in Joplin

The weather began to turn bad as the day went on. Skies had darkened again and it was now raining steadily. While ominous clouds rolled overhead, we had received word that the Governor of Missouri, Jay Nixon, was arriving in town in mid-afternoon for a press conference at the National Guard Armory. We agreed to move our press conference to 3:30 p.m. and hold it indoors at the armory location in cooperation with the one being held by the Governor. I had asked an elected state official about the governor's tendencies regarding timeliness. He indicated that he typically ran a little late. So I chose the 3:30 p.m. time slot with the expectation that Governor Nixon would want to tour the storm site in order to be better prepared to respond to questions at the press conference.

My recollection of that Monday was that the governor arrived in Joplin from the capitol in Jefferson City at approximately 2:30 p.m. By approximately 2:45 p.m., he was at the state safety mobile command center at the police annex toward the south part of the city. I went immediately there to meet with the governor at the large travel trailer type vehicle serving as the command center.

I had met Governor Nixon on two previous occasions, but had never had an opportunity to work closely with him, nor his staff. And working with him was the goal in mind as I approached this first encounter. I shook hands with the governor and we had a small exchange about the magnitude of the tornado. I then informed him of how we had changed the press conference to allow him time to tour the debris field. He looked past me, at a rather young guy, who I assumed was his chief-of-staff. The young staffer quickly responded, "No, we'll be going straight to the armory."

I was a bit surprised. I had just assumed the governor would want to view the damage before making public comment.

After the governor and I exchanged a few more words about the storm, I made my way through the rain to find Mitch, who had driven me there and was waiting in the fire department's SUV. We spent the time I had planned to show the tornado's aftermath to the governor by driving around and taking a closer look ourselves at the progress being made. We arrived at the armory, well in advance of the scheduled press conference.

I learned that the governor followed a strict plan for preparing for any public appearance. After arriving on site, he chooses to huddle with his staff in a sort of "holding room" where he receives information and facts about a particular situation or topic and the type of audience he'll be addressing. I had seen this process a few months before when Governor Nixon visited one of our wastewater plants to announce a low interest loan for a construction project at that location.

While the governor met with his personal staff in the "holding room," Lynn Onstot had convened with the governor's press staff and they informed her that the governor would lead off the press conference. She relayed that information to me and I responded, "Lynn, we will be following the *same* format as the early morning conference. I will start the 3:30 press conference by reading a prepared statement, and then the governor can say whatever he wants before taking questions."

When all participants met in the holding room prior to the press conference I made the same statement directly to the governor and his staff.

I wasn't trying to be difficult, but we had set a pattern by which we wanted the media and public to be informed. Since Governor Nixon was coming to our town and we had moved our press conference to accommodate him, I strongly suggested that we continue the format already established. There was silence for a moment, then, to his credit, the governor nodded his head in agreement.

At exactly 3:30 p.m. the Mayor, Governor Nixon, Fire Chief Randles, and myself marched single file to the front of the large room at the National Guard Armory located at 32nd Street in the southwestern part of city. I was shocked at the phalanx of reporters and photographers waiting. Over a hundred and fifty news personnel were packed into the room. In fact, I never recall seeing that many at a White House press conference. I stepped to the podium struggling to find a space to place my statement, because of all the microphones, recording devices, and wires that had been placed around the podium.

I started the press conference on a somber note by providing the latest number of confirmed fatalities due to the storm. At the close of the statement, I introduced Governor Nixon, who spoke highly of our efforts for recovery and pledged the full support of the state to Joplin and her citizens.

At this point in time, I had been up over 24 straight hours dealing with the Joplin crisis. I was in the same clothes and hat as when I left my house the previous afternoon. I would hear from family members and friends in other parts of the country as they had been following the event. They would see me being interviewed, conducting press conferences, and in photos taken of me during this time.

"Mark, we saw you on television. You looked pretty bad," they offered.

I would tell them that I looked better than I felt.

Every Eye Was on the Clouds

The weather continued to worsen as day turned into evening on May 23rd. The unthinkable had happened and now, the city was under more threats of storms. I was informed by Keith Stammer, the emergency management coordinator; Joplin was currently under a tornado warning. *There is no way we can withstand another tornado*, I thought as I heard the news. Keith also told Mitch and me that the tornado the night before had taken out three of Joplin's thirty-two warning sirens. He had hurriedly ordered three portable replacements, which were in place by early evening. That was the good news: the bad news was that one siren near the storm ravaged high school would need to be activated in the field. All tornado warning sirens are activated at a central location, usually from a 911 emergency call center. The temporary siren mounted on a trailer near the high school would need to be activated in the field.

Keith reported a possibility of 70 mile per hour winds headed our way. I silently wondered, *Lord, what would happen to the debris with those kinds of winds?* We knew there were residents still living in homes to the south of the high school that wouldn't be alerted to another incoming storm unless someone was out there to activate the siren. I turned to Mitch, "I'm going out there to operate that siren if necessary. I don't expect you to go and I'm not ordering you to go."

We had seen and been through so much in the last twenty four hours, I just couldn't ask Mitch to accompany me, given the risk. We were both bone-tired but somehow we mustered the energy required to meet every tense moment. He looked back at me and without hesitation, said, "Let's go."

"Tornado Warning! Please Take Cover!"

It was approximately 8:00 p.m. and a strange calm had enveloped the city. Mitch drove his red SUV through the rain and parked right next to the football field, south of the high school. Facing south, we monitored the western front of the city and listened to the weather forecast updates. It was dark by now, but the headlights and intermittent lightning lit up the horizon. There was nothing but destruction and debris, as far as we could see.

I cracked the window slightly and was overcome by the eeriness. There was not another person in sight. It seemed almost like we had landed on another planet and we were the only two people left alive. It was that quiet; that strange. I remember telling Mitch that I would probably jump through the roof if someone came up behind us.

I had called my wife, Lois, and told her Joplin was under another tornado warning. Our house had no electricity earlier, but Lois said service had been restored. She also told me that her whole family was there taking shelter in our home's basement, which gave me a sense of comfort to know they were safe.

Mitch and I had been parked at the high school for about a half an hour or so, when we received the order by radio to activate the sirens. Mitch hit the button that would activate the siren, but nothing happened. He then drove over to the parking lot where the trailer with the siren was located and we both jumped out and took turns pressing the button, doing whatever we could to get the portable siren working, but to no avail.

"We've got to let these residents know we are under a tornado warning," I said plaintively. Mitch looked down at the space between our two seats and replied,

"Hey, the radio works as a PA system!"

"Okay, you drive and I will use the PA."

At a high rate of speed, we tore through the neighborhood to the southeast of the high school. I began to shout into the car's PA, "Tornado warning! Please take cover! Tornado warning, please take cover!" Poor Mitch had to listen to me repeat those words over and over as we drove up and down the streets, but it worked—the folks were warned.

Luckily, Joplin was spared a second tornado in a twenty-seven hour time span. However, later that night we would learn of another related tragedy resulting from the tornado. First Responder, Jefferson Taylor III, of the Riverside, Missouri Police Department was felled by lightening after returning to his post at the intersection of 26th and Connecticut. Officer Taylor courageously fought for his life for a number of days following the tornado but, became yet another victim of the storm when he passed away on June 3rd.

The President Comes To Joplin

"I am heartbroken by the images I have seen ... All of America cares about you."

—President, Barak Obama, May 24th, 2012

Our primary focus during those first few days following the most devastating tornado our country had seen in more than sixty years was to rescue anyone still trapped in the extensive rubble. Crews had worked continually through the night of Sunday, May, 22nd searching for signs of life in the debris field.

By approximately 2:00 Monday morning, May 23rd, the federally-sponsored Missouri Task Force 1, out of Columbia, Missouri was on site with fifty people and five dog teams. They focused their search efforts at the Home Depot store and the Wal-Mart on Rangeline Road: both businesses had been destroyed by the storm. Rangeline Road runs north and south and is the heart of the city's main commercial area, on the eastern edge of the city.

I came to understand that search dogs with their hypersensitive sense of smell was the only efficient means of finding survivors in a debris field this significant. In the next few days, we would have in excess of 50 canine search units deployed in Joplin through out the time of our peak search efforts.

FEMA Arrives in Joplin

Very soon after the tornado, representatives from the Federal Emergency Management Agency (FEMA) arrived in Joplin and reported to the EOC. Never having dealt with the agency myself, I wasn't sure what to expect. I had loosely followed the Katrina disaster in August of 2005 and the stories, many of them negative, regarding FEMA's response.

The EOC had become inundated with people coming in and out constantly, including outside agencies, volunteers, and city employees. During those first days we were also busy conducting tours to the tornado site for elected officials who represented the Joplin area and surrounding areas. Early on, both United States Senators from Missouri, Roy Blunt and Claire McCaskill, visited us at the EOC. They expressed earnest concern for Joplin and pledged to help in any way they could.

FEMA Administrator, Craig Fugate, accompanied Senator McCaskill on her visit. I spoke to Mr. Fugate for some length discussing our situation. He had been the Director of the Florida Division of Emergency Management and we discussed the mutual acquaintances we had from my time in Florida as the city manager of Punta Gorda, Florida. At one point, I had opportunity to pull Mr. Fugate aside and draw upon his past experience in responding to natural disasters. It proved to be a very helpful conversation.

"Mr. Fugate, when do we make the decision to call off the search for survivors?" I asked in a most somber tone. "At what point does the operation need to change from rescue to recovery?"

This was not a decision I was looking forward to, of course, realizing there were many praying for miracles. They would hold to the hope of seeing their loved ones survive against all odds. He gave me some very sound and practical advice.

"Well, the important thing is to never give up hope. Even when it seems impossible that anyone could still be alive, you keep "spotters" in place until the last bit of debris has been removed. People who were closely watching the debris as it was loaded into the trucks were referred to as "spotters." The spotters would call a halt to loading efforts if something drew their attention until they could determine what the point of interest was. By doing so, you are prepared for an eleventh hour rescue should the opportunity occur." Mr. Fugate's insight made a lot of sense to me and I immediately incorporated that approach into our media reports and press releases.

Late Monday night, after forty straight hours, I finally fell into bed for a few hours sleep. I was emotionally and physically drained.

I Didn't Throw the President Under the Bus

During the first few days following the tornado, we tried to hold two press conferences a day to accommodate the growing demand for information sought by the national and local press. The death toll continued to rise and that information was the central point of interest for each press conference. In fact, we also received international attention on the evening of Monday, May 23rd.

As mentioned in the previous chapter, Mitch and I had made the trip through the neighborhood near the high school, alerting citizens of the tornado warning that had been issued. Afterward, I had a phone interview with the British Broadcasting Company (BBC). The reporter asked questions related to the storm, but then his questions became more political in nature as he suggested that President Obama, who was attending a conference overseas, should be returning home immediately to deal with the crisis in Joplin. It was apparent the reporter wanted me to agree that the President needed to be here on site rather than where he was at the time. After adjusting to his accent (and I'm sure he was adjusting to mine), I sidestepped any attempt to criticize the President, saying, "The President has a schedule to keep and I do not expect him to drop everything and fly to Joplin. I'm sure; he will get here whenever he can."

Communicate, Cooperate, and Follow Through

I needed all my department heads in order to organize an effective response, but I was missing one. Leslie Jones, our Finance Director, was stuck at the San Antonio, Texas Airport. She had just flown there earlier that weekend to attend an annual conference. Unfortunately, we could not get her an immediate flight back home to Joplin. She finally joined our efforts on Tuesday, May 24th. We held staff meetings nearly everyday in the training room of the main EOC room. The reports from each department head provided me with information necessary to coordinate efforts in the most hectic of circumstances. In retrospect, having everyone there and engaged, was one of the keys to our success in handling the overall response to the tornado. It also gave us a chance to instill the team approach and build morale in a situation that demanded so much. Most of us were physically exhausted.

Although I was careful not to lose sight of the loss of life and property Joplin had experienced, I tried to inject humor when appropriate to lighten the mood a little. On Sunday night while working to remove debris at the church mentioned earlier, I had received a small cut to my left hand. It was only a little two inch scrape, not serious in any way. A worker in our Health Department was giving tetanus shots to those working on the debris. I became the target of some kidding as I reluctantly rolled up my sleeve to receive my tetanus shot. I suppose even the tiniest of injuries could have become infected.

I had a poster created with the words "Communicate, Coordinate, and Follow Through," and it was placed on the wall where we held our meetings. Those three words would serve as guidance for our combined on-going efforts.

Declaration of Emergency

One of the important things we did right after the storm was to ask the mayor, Mike Woolston, to sign an emergency declaration. This enabled me to have expanded administrative authority to oversee recovery efforts. In Joplin's by-laws, the Mayor is the titular head of the city, but has no administrative authority. He or she is elected to the position by a vote of all nine members of Council and runs the council meetings and votes on legislation much like the other eight members. Mike was very visible at the EOC in the days and weeks following the tornado. He was very mindful of the limitations of his office, which enabled the EOC to operate fully without the impact of local politics. He represented the city well in the interviews he conducted, even considering his utterance to Anderson Cooper, of CNN, that we in Joplin weren't going to let this storm "kick our ass." I teased Mike the next day after the Cooper show that his mother had called and she was waiting for him at her house with a bar of soap intended for his mouth.

The Dogs Are Never Wrong

It was still Tuesday of that week when the Mayor joined Mitch (the Fire Chief) and me to once again view the storm damaged area. We climbed into Mitch's SUV and started over by St. John's hospital and traveled east, following the path of the storm. I vividly recall, Mitch stopping at the intersection of 26th and Connecticut Ave, where an apartment complex on the southeast corner laid in ruins. The charred smell of burnt debris filled the air as we made our way through the rubble. There were also fires all over town due to ruptured gas lines. I peered into the twisted wreckage of automobiles, while stepping carefully through what was left of the complex. I prayed I wouldn't see more deceased victims in one of those battered vehicles. It was hard to imagine *anyone* emerging alive from the massive piles; evidence of the destructive force of the storm.

Following our look around the area of 26th and Connecticut, we climbed back into Mitch's vehicle and continued eastward to Rangeline Road to where the Home Depot and Wal-mart store had been. We saw that dog teams were being released to search the rubble that remained. We took the opportunity to personally thank the handlers at the site, while stopping to pet some of the dogs resting nearby.

"How accurate are the animals?" I asked one of the handlers.

"They are never wrong," the female trainer said, "but, sometimes, we, their human partners err in interpreting the signals the dogs are sending." I thought how interesting that analysis was. We would be more than grateful for the tireless efforts of the canine units.

Only Half of Homes Destroyed or Damaged Had Insurance Coverage

Mitch and I would travel the storm path area at various intervals following the tornado to test the decisions made at the EOC. The EOC was very much like a bunker not only in appearance (having been built in the '60's), but, it was the space we retreated to for reporting, and assessing information. We got out of there as often as possible to see firsthand how effective our rescue and recovery efforts were working.

On these trips, invariably we would remark that it was difficult to get your bearings while in the field, as all the street signs were gone, and most, if not all of the buildings. As a result, you had little help when pinpointing a location in the hardest hit areas. Even lifelong Joplin residents made this observation. Streets and neighborhoods, once familiar, looked foreign and strange. From Rangeline Road west to St. Johns Hospital, a distance of approximately 5 miles, there was nothing to impede your view; just flattened earth and rubble.

That first week following the storm, Joplin saw an ever-increasing flow of people requesting meetings to discuss a number of issues. Some wanted just to offer assistance, others brought information about state or federal programs that could be of benefit, and some were requesting specific help for a situation resulting from the tornado. Some of these meetings, I called, and others were generated by people from the community wanting a few minutes of my time. Although, I'm sure I wasn't aware of all the meeting requests, those that did get into see me were very respectful of my time, realizing the many challenges with which we had been presented.

At one of these meetings, the head of our Planning Department, Troy Bolander informed me that the State's Department of Insurance had told him that only 57% of the households in the storm-damaged area had insurance. I was shocked! I knew this would make our rebuilding efforts much more difficult. Members of my staff offered a simple explanation in that some people could not afford it; and in the tornado damaged area, there were a high percentage of rental homes. Landlords most likely paid off the properties, but underinsured them or didn't insure them at all, never dreaming such a catastrophic event would occur.

The Tornado Left Behind Unforgettable Images

During that first week, I would discover one of the most startling facts related to the storm. The City of Joplin lost twenty-nine manhole covers in the storm-damaged area. Anyone that has tried to lift a manhole lid as a kid knows how heavy they are. I was told the average lid weighs about 200 pounds; moreover they are flush with the ground. The force of nature that could pick up something that heavy and at ground level was unimaginable.

The single most visible indication of the power of this tornado, other than the sheer overall devastation, was the sight of twisted signs, metal, and building materials flung up into the macabre looking trees. One of those trees remains vivid in my memory. The tree sat on the southern entrance to the Wal-Mart on Rangeline Road. When Mitch and I first approached the tree from the side entrance, we couldn't tell what it was that had enveloped the tree. The tree, like most in the storm-damaged area, had been debarked by the force of the tornado. What remained was a stem of stripped white wood. As we approached the tree, we were able to discern the tree was wrapped in metal from an SUV of an indeterminate make or model. One end of the vehicle's metal frame had crossed the other, with the middle of the car directly on the trunk of the tree. It brought to mind history lessons of when General Sherman ordered Union troops to bow-tie the railroad rails on the march to the sea late in the Civil War. It strained one's imagination to think of the wind force that created such a circumstance.

Joplin: Cut in Two

I thought it was important that first week to get all the city council members out on a tour to view the entire six miles of storm damage, to give them perspective on the magnitude of what we were dealing with. I knew myself that things would never be the same in Joplin and wanted to make sure that they realized that too, based on the extent of the damage. I asked my administrative assistant, Vicki Coots, to set this visits up those tours with the police department. Three of the nine, including the Mayor, had been regular visitors at the EOC. I was sure, based on conversations I had with them, that they had an appreciation for the situation and what it would mean for our future. Three of the remaining six took the tour and got to see the circumstances we were dealing with.

As the week went on, my staff had the opportunity to start amassing information detailing the extent of the damage. By late day Monday, a map had been developed showing the route of the storm. Staff had nicknamed it "the fish" given the appearance of the storm-damage area overlaid on a map of the entire city.

These are some of the facts we knew at this point: On the evening of May 22nd, a triple vortex tornado had formed on the very western edge of the city, traveling north-easterly and picking up speed as it went. It stayed on the ground, cutting a swath nearly a mile wide at spots through the area just south of the center of the city. It slowly traveled some six miles to the eastern edge of the city and into Duquesne, a small town directly east of Joplin. It appears the tornado strengthened in intensity, going from EF4 to EF5 category winds around Maiden Lane as it approached St. John's Regional Hospital and Cunningham Park, effectively cleaving the city in two. Seventy-five hundred homes were impacted, with three thousand five hundred of them destroyed or rendered uninhabitable. Five hundred businesses were destroyed or damaged. We were not sure as yet of the number of injuries or deaths resulting from the tornado. We would soon begin to give the death count at each press conference but, the number of those injured would not be provided until later in the process. Our 50,175 residents of Joplin, Missouri had just experienced the defining moment of our lives.

The day after the storm I had called our city planner, Troy Bolander, and directed him to lock his staff in a room and tell them to think of ways to plan the rebuilding of a third of our city. Some of this early work was utilized later on our recovery efforts. Troy only has three planners other than himself, so he didn't need a very big room.

Preparing for the President's Visit and the Westboro Church

We heard towards the end of the week that President Obama would be visiting Joplin that Sunday, May 29th. He was returning home from a conference in Europe and would be stopping in Joplin before returning to Washington D.C. He was to tour the debris area and then travel to the campus of Missouri Southern State University, on the north edge of the city, to address the crowd. I had been invited by the governor's staff to attend the ceremony and join the entourage on the dais. I was a little disappointed that only two department heads; the police chief and the fire chief, had been extended invitations to the event at the university. However, like most anyone would be, I was excited about the prospect of meeting the President.

As mentioned, I had been working side by side with a group of fifteen department heads and other city personnel for a solid week and felt bad that they all were not invited to participate in the event. After much thought, I decided my place was in the storm-damaged city surrounded by the department heads instead of accompanying the President to the college. I knew that visits by high-ranking federal officials were subject to last minute changes and often difficult to calculate for precise scheduling. My thought process was dictated by the work at hand: If I got a chance to meet President Obama then great, if not, than at least I had not misplaced my priorities. It was a priority check that I would have to make many times in the next few months, given the press interest, the glow of the klieg lights and the continuing presence of celebrities and officials that would descend on Joplin.

Sunday, May 29th would be a busy day in Joplin. Not only would we experience a Presidential visit, we planned to observe a moment of silence at 5:41 p.m. at Cunningham Park; indicating that it had been exactly one week since the tornado had ripped through Joplin. To further complicate things, the President's visit had made Joplin a target for activity from a group by the Westboro Baptist Church. This independent church, headquartered in Topeka, Kansas is a protest group known for picketing funerals of military casualties, burning of the American flag, and for their vehement anti-gay positions. We knew that the presence of the Westboro church would be inflammatory and distracting; not what Joplin needed during this time. We were also receiving reports that the motorcycle group, the Patriot Guard, comprised of mostly veterans would be there to counter the effects of the Westboro group. I knew it was going to be a long day, at the end of a long week in Joplin.

A group of about 15 city employees, most of whom were the department heads, boarded a bus to travel to the intersection of 22nd and Grand, just west of the battered Joplin High School. We stood in the street, surrounded by the storm damage at the intersection and awaited an opportunity to meet the President. There was advance security in the area following a routine that undoubtedly accompanies every presidential visit. Secret Service agents and city police sealed off the perimeter and federal agents, including a canine unit, inspected the nearby streets seeking out anything suspicious.

Our initial waiting place for the President's arrival was a location towards the high school next to what remained of a small brick apartment building. There, a group of the neighbors from the surrounding area joined us recounting their stories of how they survived the storm. To the south of this spot, a Joplin police officer stood by the open door of his cruiser, talking to a secret service agent. In an instant, I saw that he received a radio transmission and he tore out of his spot at a high rate of speed, spinning gravel in his wake. Standing a couple of blocks away, I knew that something was happening, most likely at the college and he had been summoned to help. I felt an uneasiness and thought to myself: *An EF5 tornado one week followed by a riot at Missouri Southern. What else could happen?*

I waited a few minutes and called Chief Roberts. He informed me that only one member of the Westboro Baptist Church group had made it to the campus and he had been confronted by a group that wasn't happy to see him. Their reaction posed a threat to the man's safety. A canister of mace had been deployed by one Police Department to diffuse the situation, then, the sole church member was escorted out of town by police. I would learn later that other Westboro church members had been surrounded by a group of citizens, including bikers from the Patriot Guard, at a nearby gas station, preventing them from getting to the university campus.

The President Tours the Tornado Zone

Shortly after talking with Chief Roberts, our group saw the president's motorcade on a street northeast of where we were and we all walked up the incline of the street to the next intersection. There was a Secret Service agent at that intersection awaiting the Presidential group's arrival on foot. Although, stoicism is their trademark, some of the department heads had engaged the agent in conversation prior to my arrival. The agent stated he had surveyed the destruction, then added, 'I've been at a lot of disasters around the country in the past ten years or so as part of my official duties; none of those compared to what I've seen in Joplin."

We looked to the north and caught glimpses of the President on foot, along side Mayor Woolston, followed by Governor Nixon. The group was talking to residents as they made their way south to the intersection where we stood.

As they neared the intersection, Mayor Woolston introduced me to President Obama and I, in turn, introduced my department heads to him saying, "Mr. President, these are the people who are going to help rebuild Joplin." He proceeded to shake each of our hands and then asked for his photographer to take a group shot with all of us.

I could see the strain of travel had burdened President Obama's tired face, yet he was very gracious to us as we offered details about the storm just before continuing his walk through the hard hit area. He would then be escorted to Missouri Southern to deliver his address. I was pleased to have had the opportunity to meet the President and I could see on the faces of my department heads, they were enlivened and encouraged by the chance to meet the man that held the most powerful office in the world.

Our group all piled back in the bus and returned to the EOC to prepare for the event later that afternoon which would include honoring the victims of the tornado with a moment of silence. President Obama and Governor Nixon would journey to the Leggett and Platt Arena at the university, where both would deliver speeches, also paying tribute to the citizens that perished in the tornado and pledging to remain by the city's side through the entire storm recovery process.

A Speech for a Special Moment

I, had been up the previous night, unable to sleep and wondering what message to deliver late that afternoon to the citizens of Joplin. Standing on my front porch, at 3 a.m. in the morning, I prayed to God for inspiration, "Please, give me words that will not only heal, but also encourage those who have been through so much."

I usually preferred a structured approach to public speaking, like the text I read word-for-word at the press conference held earlier that week. In this instance, I opted for an outline of general points and decided to draw the specific words from my heart. By the time I stepped to the microphone that afternoon, I had worked over 120 hours that first week. Pure adrenaline was keeping me upright. Given the level of fatigue I was feeling, I needed the structure of the outline in case I lost my way, but I felt the need to express raw emotion. The speech could have one of two results: it could be helpful for the community or could prove to be a big mistake.

Shortly after 5:00 p.m., citizens and staff once again gathered at the parking lot at Cunningham Park facing the battered St. John's Hospital to the south. We had been sent a song earlier in the week that had been given to us by a songwriter from Virginia entitled "Sing Again." Our Director of Information Technology, Mark Morris, received the song first, dedicated to Joplin by the writer. The song would be played following the 5:41 p.m. moment of silence to honor our fellow citizen's who lost their lives the previous week.

I had asked Gary Shaw, the former Mayor and current city council member, to deliver a prayer. Gary is the administrator of Central Christian Church, located in our downtown area of Joplin and an overall great person. I was honored to have him play a role in this important event.

Mayor Woolston delivered some brief comments, prior to my stepping forward to the bank of microphones crowding the podium. I began by apologizing in advance to the citizens, because I knew I would have difficulty keeping my emotions in check, which proved to be true. These are some of the points I shared at that special meeting in the park:

I suggested to the citizens that the best tribute we could pay to the citizens we had lost, was to dedicate our efforts to the clean-up and rebuilding of the town to their memory. In that manner, they could continue to live on.

I also coined a phrase that described, for me and hopefully others the incredible outpouring of support and assistance Joplin had received that first week from throughout the area, region, country, and even the world. I told the audience, what we were witnessing was "The Miracle of the Human Spirit," as demonstrated by the love and compassion we had received and would continue to receive!

I shared my lifelong belief that good things can come out of bad things if you have the right attitude. I told them that 5:41 p.m., May 22nd, 2011 was the defining moment in all of our lives, whether we wanted it to be or not, and we needed to make sure that we honor the deceased memories in our efforts as we move forward.

We observed the moment of silence and then played the recording of "Sing Again." The radio station covering the ceremony included the song so Joplin and her neighbors could hear the anthem. By that time, there weren't many dry eyes in the crowd. There were probably 400-500 people in the park when we the ceremony began. My back was to the higher hills of Cunningham Park, so I was not aware that an estimated 1500-2000 additional people poured in from behind us, as we went through the program. I had more than one person tell me that the sight of citizens pouring over the rolling hill behind me, toward the park for the ceremony was the perfect metaphorical image survivors of the storm emerging from the debris following the tornado.

After the song, there was a long pause; it seemed as though people didn't know what to do. I was so focused on the earlier part of the event that I had not considered any final words. I sensed a need to say something to close the ceremony, so I stepped back to the podium and thanked people for coming and then blurted out something that just felt right, "We will rebuild and be stronger than we were before the storm. I give you my word."

Then, a man rose from the audience and began to play "Amazing Grace" on his bagpipe. He had not been part of the planned observance, but it was a fitting tribute and brought a perfect end to the emotion-packed week and a very long day.

Dealing With Human Loss At Storm Central

"My heart goes out to all the people that have been affected by the devastating Missouri tornado ... especially in my hometown of Joplin ... it is difficult to put into words, the emotions I have when I see the devastation ... my thoughts and prayers are extended to all the people who are dealing with so much loss."

—Jamie McMurray,
NASCAR Sprint Cup Driver
Following his tour of Joplin Tornado Damage

We were back at the EOC early Monday morning May 30th, eight days after the tornado that left Joplin in shambles. We had begun a routine that called for two staff meetings a day; one in the morning and another at 6 p.m. As mentioned, we were holding all press conferences at Cunningham Park. In between meetings with the staff, I had on-going meetings with individual staff members, other public officials from the state, and individuals (citizens) representing groups in the community who wanted to help in some capacity. We kept this routine up for sixteen hours a day, at what could best be described as a hectic pace.

My administrative assistant, Vicki, had approached me with a good idea on May 30th about keeping a calendar to provide some sense of structure from that point forward. Typically, I utilize a calendar to provide order to my daily schedule, but there was nothing typical about that first week after the tornado.

One of the most vivid recollections I had from Monday, May 30th was a visit I received from FEMA officials, among them, Libby Turner, their on-site leader. By that time, my office had been moved to an area directly across the hallway from the operating EOC. This was necessitated by the rush of visitors we were receiving in the training room, adjacent to the main EOC room itself. There was an outer room with a table in this new area, which was about 10 feet by 16 feet; this is where we held staff meetings. Right to the side of this room, was my office, borrowed from the Jail Supervisor. This room was about four feet wide and 8 feet long. It didn't have brooms and wash buckets stored in it, but it could have. Despite being totally devoid of charm, I was thankful for both the space and a reasonable semblance of solitude.

Libby, a courtly southern lady, was one of the first visitors to my new area and she brought welcome news. On the heels of his visit to Joplin to witness the devastation, President Obama had approved a pilot program called Expedited Debris Removal or EDR. Retroactive to May 23rd, the order stated we had 75 days from that earlier date to remove the estimated 3,000,000 cubic yards of debris under an arrangement in which the Federal Government would cover 75% of the expense necessary to cleanup Joplin. In conjunction with the Army Corps of Engineers, we had a lot of work to do between now and August 7th, 2011.

During the week of May 30th, we began series of late afternoon meetings involving the mayor and various city staff, regarding potential building code changes, in the wake of the damage caused by the tornado. In the short time since the storm, there had been a surprising amount of discussion in the city regarding the strengthening of building codes, requiring safe rooms and the reconstruction of the city governed by green principles that would assure rebuilding in smarter ways to carry us into the future.

These late afternoon discussions included the city's lead building official, Steve Cope, who was conducting ongoing research at the time the discussions were taking place. We were preparing for a special council meeting on Tuesday June 7th, when the city's elected officials were first scheduled to address these issues. Those gathered in my basement office at the EOC knew that Joplin was a conservative community, with more than a few residents who tended toward libertarian views. In addition, Joplin is not a wealthy community. All of these considerations had to be balanced against protecting future generations and doing the responsible thing in light of the circumstances with which we were dealing. We also realized that no amount of preparation in the future would be sufficient to offer protection from 200 miles per hour plus winds like Joplin experienced on May 22nd.

Helping the Homeless

We had a meeting on Wednesday, during that second week with representatives from FEMA and other housing-related organizations to discuss mid-term living accommodations for displaced Joplin citizens. We had made arrangements at the Leggett and Platt Arena at Missouri Southern State University's campus and with the Red Cross to set up a shelter to house displaced citizens immediately after the tornado. Other shelters developed at different locations to supplement our main facility at the college. This would only suffice for immediate needs. Some five hundred and three residents were housed in shelters throughout the city at our peak time on Wednesday evening May 25th, with some 348 of those individuals being housed at the Arena at MSU.

Given the fragmented nature of our circumstances, we knew residents were staying with friends and relatives and many others were utilizing the approximately 2,000 local hotel/motel units available in Joplin.

As thinly staffed as the city was, I personally attended the May 25th meeting with FEMA representatives with Planning Director, Troy Bolander. We knew going in that keeping our residents nearby would be essential to our overall goal of losing as little of Joplin's population as possible. By that point, we had heard through various sources that Greensburg, Kansas, a city to our west had lost 40% of its population after a devastating tornado they experienced in May of 2007. I had also received staff reports of New Orleans losing 35% to 40% of their population, as a result of Hurricane Katrina. Those numbers would not be acceptable in Joplin. We simply were not going to let that happen.

We walked into the Fire Department conference room on the first floor of the Safety Building, knowing only a handful of the 25 or so people in the room. Troy and I took our seats near the far east wall and following introductions of all in attendance, a discussion began about intermediate housing needs. We wanted to accommodate adults, families, and children who had been left homeless and needed alternatives in place as soon as possible.

Following major disasters, FEMA often supplies mobile homes (trailers) for those needing housing. We learned that FEMA didn't use the term "trailer," instead, referring to the units as "manufactured housing units" or (MHU's). When I asked when we could have the first MHU's on site in Joplin, the female FEMA representative stated they would be in place "by first frost." She had barely gotten the words out when I turned to her and said, "That is completely unacceptable."

This was May and to have victims without appropriate housing for four to five months until "first frost" seemed not only an unnecessary delay, but, a calloused one. I am sure I shocked some people with my response, but I was looking out for our citizens and the long-term interests of the city. Although there was an awkward silence after my comment, it was followed by a pledge from FEMA to revisit the timetable. I was glad I had spoken up. In the end, I was told by FEMA that the average turn around time for deployment of MHU's at a group site was 60 days from the day the site was approved by City Council. For Joplin, I'm happy to report, the first units rolled onto the group site located by the airport in 31 days.

Assessing our Financial Loss

One of things we started discussing early on following the tornado was the long-term financial stability of the city. There were so many needs and even more uncertainty, that we found it difficult to predict our long-term financial outlook. Although prior to May 22nd our condition was solid, I had stated early on that the city would need help from other levels of government to get through this crisis. With that thought in mind, I prepared a letter for Mayor Woolston's signature to be presented to Governor Nixon on his June 1st visit to the Joplin Chamber of Commerce offices. In that letter, we officially requested that the state pick up the remainder of the 10% cost for the Expedited Debris Removal cost. President Obama had earlier approved the federal government's payment of 90% of the debris removal (up from 75%), provided we finished before the August 7th deadline.

NASCAR's McMurray and Other Celebs Stunned by Devastation

The flood of celebrities and government officials visiting Joplin continued. On Thursday, June 2nd, NASCAR driver Jamie McMurray, winner of the 2010 Daytona 500, visited Joplin with one of the representatives of his racing team, Chip Ganassi (Earnhardt-Ganassi Racing). Johnny Morris, owner of Bass Pro Shops based in nearby Springfield, Missouri and a sponsor of the Earnhardt-Ganassi team, also accompanied Jamie on the visit. Jamie's father and mother also visited.

Jamie had a special interest in Joplin as he grew up in Duquesne, a city just a stone's throw to the east of Joplin, also hit hard by the tornado. In fact, his boyhood home had been leveled. Jamie, Chip and Johnny all appeared to be shaken by the level of destruction they had witnessed by the time I met up with them at Cunningham Park. Their comments would echo those of visitors before and after them, in that "the pictures and press accounts couldn't do justice in describing the extent of the damage." Following a short discussion, we parted ways as they continued their tour and I returned to the EOC. We would meet up again at a 3:00 p.m. for a press conference back at the Safety Center.

Following my prepared comments at the conference, I introduced Jamie. The press was very interested in Jaime's reaction to what he had seen. That was the first time I had met Jaime, but he seemed to have been profoundly impacted by the damage to his hometown, as he responded to the questions in a thoughtful and deliberate manner.

The second week after the tornado saw more celebrity visits in the EOC. Representatives from the beautiful Downstream Casino, located 4 miles west of Joplin, just inside the Oklahoma border, had been providing meals for those working in the EOC since the day following the storm. They also helped boost morale by inviting Barry Switzer, former Coach of Oklahoma Sooners from 1973-1988 and head coach of the Dallas Cowboys from 1994-1996, along with Billy Sims, Oklahoma's Heisman Trophy-winning running back, to Joplin. I remembered meeting Billy back in 1978 at the College Football Hall of Fame at Kings Island, Ohio at an autograph session. He had more than a passing interest in Joplin. Billy Sims Barbecue Restaurant is located on 7th street in Joplin, but was not damaged by the tornado. The guys came at a particularly busy time at the EOC and their visit proved to be a welcome break from the tedious, often overwhelming work we were doing day after day.

Accounting for the Missing; Identifying the Victims

Two storm related issues became real problems during that second week. First, the number of residents still unaccounted for was a real concern; and, second, identifying and releasing the deceased to loved ones proved to be a challenging process.

With the extent of the debris field, we had no idea how many people, might still be trapped beneath the rubble. Two people had been recovered alive on Tuesday, May 24th, but we had no idea, who else might still be trapped inside destroyed homes and businesses. We were continuing to utilize the dog teams to try to find anyone that might still be trapped. The Joplin Police Department had been keeping a list of potential missing persons. That list was based on calls we were receiving, word of mouth, and other sources of information. That same day one of my staff had mistakenly conveyed to a member of the press that there were 1,500 on the missing persons list, which needless to say created frenzy within the press corps. The staffer knew he had made a huge mistake that induced panic and I had a discussion with him about the importance of reporting affirmed facts.

The inference drawn from the error was that in addition to the known 122 deceased at this time, there were 1,500 still buried beneath the rubble! We immediately set about trying to mitigate the problems this report created by issuing press releases and emphasizing the error in all associated press conferences.

As stated, the establishment of a missing persons list and the entire process of identifying bodies and notifying loved ones was rapidly becoming a problem. Unfortunately, we at the city couldn't exert any control over this process. Our role in the grim task ended once bodies were found in the field and were transported to the football field parking lot at Missouri Southern State University. I had heard we were getting some negative reporting based on the challenges surrounding rescue and recovery efforts. An already slow and difficult process, nearly ground to a halt, as I was informed of a mis-identification on one of the initial bodies that was released to one of the families. That must have been a heart wrenching ordeal for the family involved.

Originally, the challenging job of identifying remains fell to the Jasper County Coroner, Rob Chappel. Joplin is a city that lies in two separate counties. No significant storm damage occurred in Newton County, located to the south of 32nd street. Shortly after the storm, it became evident that the demands of the situation were beyond the resources of the Jasper County Coroner, so a call went out to Disaster Mortuary Operational Response Team (DMORT). DMORT is a state group of private professionals steeped in mortuary science and related fields. DMORT works under the guidance of local officials by providing needed technical assistance. Included in this group are funeral directors, medical examiners, pathologists, forensic anthropologists, finger print specialists, dental assistants, and many other groups of professionals. Help from all of these disciplines was essential in order to complete the task of identifying victims.

I had been told that damage with 200 plus mile per hour winds to the human body, with associated debris and materials flying around at the same speed, could be extensive. Given the challenges involved, and at the request of the state, we began using the term "human remains" instead of "bodies" when referring to deceased victims on May 31st. In addition, we agreed to let DMORT and the State Department of Public Safety, establish the agreed upon number of human remains. Prior to that point, the city was using a number in press releases that was tracked in to the EOC, based on the findings of the search teams in the field. This number was gathered in real time, but when I found out how difficult the identification process was, we willingly shifted our approach to the release of that information. We agreed; given the challenges to use the number DMORT had released.

Later, as time went on, the morgue was relocated to a vacant munitions factory near the Jasper County Sheriff's satellite office. I never visited the DMORT operations at the college or at the sheriff's satellite office. I had already seen enough from my involvement in the rescue operations immediately following the storm; I relied on the reports received from Joplin's law enforcement personnel which emanated directly from the coroner. Those reports were received with sorrow and a whispered prayer for each victim's family and friends.

Utter Devastation

"It is utter devastation anywhere you look to the south and the east-businesses, apartment complexes, houses, cars, trees, schools, you name it, it is leveled."

—Melodee Colbert-Kean,
Joplin Mayor Pro Tem

As previously mentioned, I had met Missouri Governor, Jay Nixon, prior to his becoming governor, when he spoke at a Missouri Municipal League Conference in Jefferson City. He had just delivered a speech to the attending delegates. The speech wasn't particularly memorable that day, but, I'm no Daniel Webster myself. He then entered the hotel lobby to shake hands with members of the audience. Nixon was extremely affable as he shook our hands and I left with a positive impression based on his friendliness.

As earlier indicated, I saw him again after he became governor, when he held a press conference to announce our receiving a low-interest loan from the state to help finance some improvements to one of our wastewater plants. That would be the first of several instances where I would witness his staff using a "holding room" for the governor and his entourage when they arrived on a site. Local officials were not allowed in this room. After meeting with his personal staff, I was invited along with the Mayor and others were invited to join him in another office for about 10 minutes. Once we were all huddled together in that office, he began to recount stories of his summers when he was going to school and about his experience working construction sites; the connection being the project we were all gathered to discuss–the subject of the press conference. They were all good stories but, you could tell the governor was a little uncomfortable because he spoke rapidly and didn't give anyone else an opportunity to speak. I empathized with him because I am the world's worst at small talk.

Fast forwarding to May 23rd, the day following the tornado, I was concerned that maybe there were different motivations at play following the press conference held with the Governor at the Armory (the one in which I insisted we use the same protocol as the earlier conference.) I had been pleased when I heard Governor Nixon was coming to town and knew Joplin would require help from the state and federal government. My expectation of his arrival and visit was that the state would assist us in any way possible and respond to any request we would make.

Missouri Department of Public Safety Responsible for Accounting for the Missing

On May 26th, Governor Nixon assigned the Missouri Department of Public Safety the task of overseeing the missing person's list related to the Joplin disaster. One of the first actions of the agency was to stipulate that only relatives of a supposed missing person could report that individual as "unaccounted for" to the Missouri Highway Patrol. Although, I was not directly a part of that process, I knew this standard for reporting served to legitimize the count and gave the agency a starting point for determining and locating the missing persons. This process, no doubt helped in the DMORT's identification efforts. One of the unintended consequences of this procedure was that once this list was cleared and thought to be complete the dog search teams pulled out of the Joplin area.

We at the EOC, felt most everyone was relying too much on the state's identification process and thought there had to be some instances of people still missing, who either didn't have relatives involved in their lives and/or were transients. The very day following the list being cleared, I got an email from a lady in Michigan, who thought her son may have been in Joplin on May 22nd. I relayed the message to Fire Chief Randles, who in turn promptly called the worried mother for some background information on her son. Mitch sent search crews out to investigate her son's known friends and places he had frequented based on his conversation with the mother, but the search yielded no results. There were no dogs available, because they had been pulled out of town, so Mitch's crews conducted the search by themselves. We didn't know if he lay among the three million cubic yards of debris strewn throughout Joplin or if he was actually even in town on the afternoon of May 22nd. We didn't hear from the mother again so we assumed the young man was located and had not been in Joplin on May 22nd.

Governor's Visits Brought Good News

Governor Nixon was in Joplin often after the storm. To his credit, he did direct a significant number of resources to Joplin. His visits typically coincided with an announcement of a new source of aid to assist in our efforts. One of these announcements was to direct all of Missouri's low income housing credits for the year to Joplin because of the overwhelming immediate needs. We had 7,500 residences impacted by the storm.

As we transitioned out of the debris removal stage and into the rebuilding phase we had occasion to meet with both state officials and many developers that focused their attention on Joplin because of the tools and incentives Nixon had sent Joplin's way. One of the initial meetings in this regard was held in our second floor conference room at City Hall. By this time, we had moved to the EOC from the basement of the Safety Center to the basement of City Hall, in the heart of our redeveloped downtown. Members of the governor's staff conveyed to our Planning Director, Troy Bolander, and me, that the governor wanted to get housing started as soon as possible. Troy and I both agreed that getting housing started was a good thing, but, an updated housing study was in the process of being compiled, as well as a report due from the Citizen's Action Recovery Team (CART) composed of information gathered from Joplin's own residents as to how they would like to see Joplin rebuilt. We felt that implementing a plan before we had these reports could be a serious mistake and not in Joplin's long term interest. We could tell that was not the response they were looking for, as it wouldn't have the quick-hitting action and public appeal that we felt prompted the meeting.

Deadline Looming for Debris Removal

Toward the end of our deadline for Expedited Debris Removal (EDR) of August 7th, it was looking as though we might need an extension in order to complete the process. Most would agree that the progress made in cleaning up the debris was near miraculous, given the massive amount with which we had to contend. The piles of debris were largely gone, hauled away to four nearby landfills, but the efforts had slowed since the Army Corp of Engineers had changed contractors in early July. That transition, along with the properties that had asbestos concerns had slowed progress. The city had requested an extension of the deadline, since we really weren't given a full 75 days. President Obama had authorized the EDR process on the 29th of May retroactive to May 23rd based on the retroactive enactment, we really only had 68 days to complete the task. The extension we had requested had to go through the state.

On Wednesday August 3rd, we received word that FEMA had denied our extension request. We were disappointed, but we had been meeting privately with the contractor, urging him to push his crews to complete the removal by August 7th. I had called FEMA's Deputy Administrator, Rich Serino, on August 1st, asking for his help. I had formed a bond with Rich when he had visited Joplin the first week following the tornado and wanted to see if I could use that relationship to help Joplin's citizens. It didn't work.

Governor Nixon was apparently more disappointed than I was. On Thursday afternoon August 4th, he had a press conference in the storm area in front of a lot yet to be cleared, criticizing FEMA for not granting the request and saying there was no way that we were going to make the August 7th deadline for the completion of debris removal.

I received a text on Sunday August 7th, indicating the contractor had finished his efforts on time. There was still debris at curb sites around the affected neighborhoods but, that was largely from citizens demolishing their own homes, which was the next step in the clean up process, and hauling the material to the curb for pick up. In his press conference, Nixon pledged to pick up the 25% costs that we would have born after the August 7th deadline. In reality the only remaining debris visible after the deadline was from demolished houses that had been left standing *after* the storm and not considered part of debris removal. Behind the scenes, FEMA reps were not happy with the governor's remarks.

I just can't thank the hard-working men and women enough who accomplished this seemingly impossible task of removing mountains of debris by the August 7th deadline. As a student of history, I believe it was one of the most significant post World War II logistical efforts ever accomplished on the domestic front.

Planning the Memorial Service for November

On Monday, October 3rd, I was preparing for council meeting in my office at City Hall when the phone rang and on the other end was our Parks and Recreation Director, Chris Cotten. Chris was a young man I had hired earlier in the year, who had been thrust into situations neither one of us had imagined during his interview process. He had a great attitude and at the time was focused on rebuilding Cunningham Park, the city's oldest park, where you may recall, press conferences were being held regularly. The park is located across the street from St. John's Hospital.

"Mark, a representative from the Governor's office called to tell me the governor wants five minutes of time at our memorial service on November 22nd to honor those lost in the tornado," Chris reported.

"I can't make that decision. The event is being planned by the memorial committee—it will be their call," I told Chris. The committee had been adamant that the event, to be held on November 22nd, six months after the tornado, be Joplin's day. They didn't want anything to distract from the purpose of the event, which was to create a special time for the residents of Joplin—a time to feel united in healing, and to share our common goals for the future. It was to be a special memorial in many ways.

"Don't Think it Can't Happen To You!"

"Realistically, the chance of finding someone alive is diminishing with each passing day, but we will proceed with the hope of a miracle occurring."

—Mark Rohr, City Manager, Joplin, Missouri

As of May 31st, we had discovered 146 human remains. We knew the chances of finding anyone alive at this point were remote. It had been nine days since the storm. Fire Chief, Mitch Randles and I had consulted a physician in the EOC early on in the process, who had told us, he felt an adult in good physical shape, could last no more than a week without food and water. The search teams, at the city's direction, had performed six passes of the entire storm area with the canine units and their handlers and then two additional passes with the dogs in the lead and their masters following well behind. Mitch probably thought I was crazy ordering so many swipes of the city, but I think he knew how uncomfortable I was with the prospect of suspending the search efforts and was quick to follow through in whatever was asked of him. We would also continue to do spot searches, based on information warranting such.

By this time, the debris removal process had started and we were employing the advice of FEMA's chief administrator, Craig Fugate, in that we had "spotters," employees for the Corp of Engineers, actively watching the debris being loaded into the tandem truck units in the event they spotted something that warranted closer inspection.

Police Chief, Lane Roberts had implemented a curfew on June 3rd, twelve days after the tornado. We had experienced some problems with looters and this was one of the means he had utilized to control that situation. Early on he had also attempted a registration system, requiring those wanting access to the storm-stripped area, to stipulate their need for being in the area and requiring a license to gain entry. This proved logistically difficult, to say the least, and was the source of many complaints. He abandoned the process shortly after it started. In doing so, he would refer to a comment I had made several times at press conferences that there is no "how to" book in dealing with a crisis of this magnitude.

Furthermore, the circumstances of each disaster are different and require responses specific to each event. Our situation required leadership to make a hundred or so snap judgments every day based on the information made available. However, I do believe there are some general tenets of emergency response that need to be observed, in order to deal with the myriad of challenges an EF5 tornado or other similar disaster presents.

Get Organized

I prioritized the needs for recovery and came up with Ten Tenets for Disaster Recovery. # 1 Tenet–When dealing with wide spread disaster get organized. Have a room where you can think and gather your thoughts and tend to the many things for which you will be responsible. You may have to perform a kind of bureaucratic triage in order to achieve that organization. Certain meetings or topics you just won't have time for; you will either have to say no as to your participation, or delegate others to represent you.

Also, as mentioned previously, be mindful of the fact that different people respond differently to stress. Some curl up in a figurative catatonic ball, and will be of little help to you, while others kick it up an extra gear or two as the exigencies of the situation demand. It will be clearly evident to you, who fits in which category in short order.

Tenet #2 of disaster response is to understand there will be trial and error involved. Don't be afraid to implement something that makes sense; and just as important, don't be afraid to abandon the idea if it doesn't work. Clinging to a failed policy or approach, out of stubbornness or pride doesn't do any good in a crisis of this magnitude and in fact threatens to overshadow the other successful attributes of your efforts.

Update of Housing Efforts

On Monday June 6th at 9:00 A.M., we had another housing meeting in the Fire Department's conference room which provided an update of the housing efforts. I was informed that many families left homeless were staying with relatives or friends, some were staying at local hotels or shelters and, others were starting to use FEMA financial assistance to fill up a limited supply of local rental units. I was also pleased to learn that the process for manufactured housing units had started and that the first of these units would be in Joplin shortly. Prior to these manufactured houses (Mobile Housing Units, MHU's) being located at a group site, all available area commercial pads would have to be filled. How many MHU's, we would need at that point was the source of speculation. FEMA was contacting those families who had registered with them on an ongoing basis to determine their needs and directing people accordingly.

Town Hall Meeting to Discuss FEMA Requirements

We were scheduled to have a Town Hall meeting at the Taylor Performing Arts Center on the campus of Missouri Southern State University the night of Monday, June 6th. Typically, we have a council meeting the first and third Monday of every month, but had cancelled the meeting that week. The purpose of *this* town hall meeting was to provide impacted residents information on housing opportunities and to discuss the debris removal process in greater detail. It would also be the first time that Right of Entry forms would be available. The forms, signed by property owners, gave the Army Corps of Engineers contractors access to clean the debris off their lots. Accompanying this was a rather complicated explanation of the reimbursement procedure property owners would have to follow, so as not to receive both the debris removal help from the Army Corps, and insurance settlement monies to cover that operation.

We had created a reimbursement schedule, working with FEMA, which was made up of categories prorated according to lot size. The bottom line was that homeowners couldn't get insurance money for debris that FEMA removed, as it was considered double dipping. Homeowners were required to reimburse FEMA if insurance covered the cost of removing the debris– the larger the lot, the larger the reimbursement.

I was a little nervous about the meeting, not because of the 2,000 or so people in attendance, but, rather because I hadn't seen a video to be presented that evening. The video had been created in nearby Springfield depicting the debris removal process, but had been completed just moments before the meeting. I had delegated its development to Leslie Jones, the Finance Director, and, to a lesser degree, Public Information Officer, Lynn Onstot. I was anything but a micromanager, but, I didn't like surprises either. The video was shown and helped to give a visual image of the process, but, there were still lingering questions.

The meeting itself went well, but, as stated, I was sure there remained many questions in the minds of impacted residents. I was careful to mention how important our citizens were to rebuilding the city and how vital it was that those in attendance continue to call Joplin home, as we worked through this difficult process. I had been lobbied by some of my staff to open the floor up to questions and answers. I was reluctant to do so, because of the uncontrolled nature of such a process, however, I relented—and later wished I hadn't.

The meeting got a bit sloppy at the end when an environmentalist grabbed the mike to say that he personally wanted to *recycle* the 3 million cubic yards of debris! His speech was something the pragmatic storm victims had little patience for at the moment. After the event, the department heads and I went down into the crowd where we handed out stuffed animals people had donated as gifts to the children in the audience. I received valuable input from the citizens in the audience as I stopped to listen to their needs, one-on-one, that evening.

Increase in Business for Landfill Owners

The following day was like the many before, full of meetings and phone calls. My assistant, Public Works Director, Jack Schaller, was one of my employees that really rose to the occasion. Jack and Leslie, the Finance Director, emerged as the two staff members that handled the debris removal process as a whole. Jack had informed me that one of the three landfills that we were using in nearby Kansas was being flexible with their tipping fees. This is a fee charged by landfill operators for dumping each truck load, based on weight. I had very little patience with this type of behavior having remarked earlier that all four landfill owners, (the last one located to our north in Lamar, Missouri) had to be making a large fortune with the remains of 1/3 of our city heading their way. I immediately called the Attorney General in Kansas to request the favor of their attention on this matter. I received a prompt phone call back and I never heard a complaint again on the landfill rates.

Two Weeks Out; Agenda Points for Council Meeting

The following evening we had a work session scheduled with the City Council. It had been over two weeks since the tornado and it was time to talk about some policy decisions that were developing. There were a number of things on the agenda that evening. One of the most important things that had come up was the possible changes to our building codes, in light of the EF5 tornado.

There had been some public discourse about the potential of requiring safe rooms in residential homes going forward. There weren't many basements in Joplin because of our rocky soil. A safe room is a smaller, concrete reinforced structure that could be included or added to the structure of the home for approximately $5,000, where inhabitants of the home can go to ride out a storm. I wasn't surprised, given the overall libertarian nature of some of our citizens, that there wasn't a lot of support for mandating safe rooms. There was however, a great deal of positive discussion about requiring hurricane straps, which would fasten roof trusses to the frame of the house and more frequent frame connections to the initial block section of a foundation, as well as filling the base of block cavities with concrete to offer more stability for homes constructed in the future. The subject of a building moratorium was also discussed. Staff felt that given the deadline for debris removal and the number of large trucks that would be operating in that area, it wouldn't be safe or efficient to have construction crews in the same zone. Although this proved to be a controversial issue, I felt most people agreed with the idea of delaying rebuilding.

Janet Napolitano, Secretary of Homeland Security, Scheduled to Visit Joplin

The following day, Wednesday June 8th, was when the Secretary of Homeland Security, Janet Napolitano, was scheduled to arrive in Joplin along with Shawn Donovan, Secretary of Housing and Urban Development. Both had to cancel at the last minute, but Secretary Napolitano would return to Joplin twice in the near future. Prior to this visit, a local businessman had invited representatives from DR Horton, one of the largest home builders in the country, to meet with a group of local officials and leaders in Joplin. At lunchtime, United States Congress Representatives, Billy Long and Lynn Jenkins attended our staff meeting held in the lunchroom of the EOC building. There we discussed the prospect of declaring the entire storm area, a "distressed zone," to qualify for tax credits.

The Red Cross Said What?

Sometime during that third week, an issue had developed with the Red Cross. I never really had an occasion in my career to deal with the Red Cross at least to the magnitude that we had to do so now. Each morning I came into my office at the EOC at the Safety Center where typically around 50 emails received overnight would be awaiting my response. On one particular morning, one of these emails was from my assistant, Sam, who had received a call from someone interested in volunteering who was told by a Red Cross representative that we did not need any more volunteers. I was not happy.

This leads to the Tenet #3 of disaster response: Find a way for everyone to participate, either by donating or volunteering. By adhering to that principle we were able to build widespread support and produce some staggering volunteer numbers in the process. Most people want to help their fellow man and this approach enabled them to do so. We wanted to give people an opportunity to help; to feel they were a part of history by aiding the victims of such a monumental crisis.

I called Debi Meeds, who was heading up the local Red Cross operations and expressed to one of her assistants my displeasure that their staff had basically told the world, "Joplin doesn't need any more help." I was averaging about 16 hours a day since the tornado and I'm sure some of my weariness played out in that phone call. Debbi came to see me later that afternoon to explain the statement issued by the Red Cross was indeed in error.

"Mark, it was a stupid comment and I will get it straightened out immediately." I couldn't fathom anyone perceiving we had suddenly run out of work to do and had no further need for volunteers. Despite this problem, the Red Cross was doing a lot to assist Joplin in the aftermath of the storm.

The Storm's Violence Impacted our Young Son, Ryan

I learned another valuable lesson that week. Late one evening that week my wife brought our two kids up to the EOC to spend time with their dad. Ryan, 4, and Riley, almost 3, were glad to see me. We spent some time drawing pictures and playing around in my office area before we went home. It was starting to turn dark that evening as Lois and I fastened them in their safety seats in my car. They were always riding around with mom and wanted to ride in my car for a change. Lois wanted to go to the Expedited Debris Removal (EDR) area to see the house where she used to live near Parr Hill Park. I agreed to follow her. I looked at the kids in the rearview mirror as we would wind through the streets in the damaged area. Riley, being so young, was oblivious to her surroundings. However, Ryan, our four year old, is a quiet, introspective kid whose eyes were as big as half-dollars as he stared out the window at the wreckage of the only town he has ever known. I wondered what he was thinking. It wasn't long until I found out.

Lois had detoured off the route to run an errand, and I headed home. As soon as we got out of the car Ryan said, "Daddy, I don't feel good."

I followed him to the restroom where he promptly threw-up. The little guy was not sick, but apparently had an upset stomach due to the overwhelming disaster he had witnessed. I was saddened to think about the impact that the tornado had on Joplin's youngest citizens. Ryan had seen so much those past two weeks, and would possibly never forget the night of the storm itself.

Like Spitting in the Ocean

Thursday June 9th, was also a very long day. I couldn't sleep very well the previous night so I got up at 5:30 A.M., dressed and made my way over to the storm damaged area near the high school. It was now 6 a.m. and I had some time before I had to be at the office, so I picked a spot at some property nearby and methodically began to clear some debris, taking time to separate materials at the curb. I was there about 15 minutes when one of our police officers pulled up. He probably thought I was a looter. I approached his cruiser and leaned in, "Just wanting to help out a while," I said, "but, really, it's like spitting in the ocean."

I do not know if he knew who I was or not, but either way, he had to think I was crazy being up that early, clearing a lot. Apparently satisfied that I wasn't doing anything illegal, the officer simply said, "Well, stay safe," then resumed his patrol.

Don't Get Seduced by the Limelight!

Later that morning, I accompanied the Mayor and Fire Chief to the Joplin Regional Airport to greet Secretary of Homeland Security Napolitano, who landed for her initial visit, previously noted in this chapter. Homeland Security was the department, which oversees FEMA's operations. On the tarmac I couldn't get close to the Secretary due to other local officials and state representatives surrounding her, jockeying for position. Nothing against Secretary Napolitano, because I came to view her as a true and genuine person in the time I got to talk with her in person, but I was a little put off by the political fawning from some who greeted her at the airport.

I knew managing this disaster, was not about entertaining visiting dignitaries or, mugging for the cameras of the national media but, about truly helping those in need. Mad at myself for having to realize a lesson I had already learned, I exited the motorcade escorting Secretary Napolitano from the airport at the red light at 4th and Rangeline, deciding to walk back to do work at the EOC. Looking back, I was probably lucky not to have drawn the attention of some black helicopters, but, I wanted to get back to doing my real job as soon as possible. That is the fourth tenet of disaster management: Don't get seduced by the limelight and vast attention; stay focused on what is important, which is to help the citizens in need.

My walk back to the EOC was shortened when my wife, who was in the area, picked me up and drove me back to the EOC after I had trekked about a-third of a mile. Once back at the office, Troy Bolander and I tried to reach Jonathan Reckford, CEO of Habitat International in Atlanta, Georgia.

We were told he was on vacation but were able to speak to Bonnie, his assistant. I told Bonnie we needed help as we had 7,500 houses impacted by the tornado. The conversation ended with our expectation that Habitat International would be working on a plan to assist Joplin. While the local affiliates have been great, I am still waiting on that call from Habitat International.

We Made Time to Attend a Funeral—One of Many

Later that same day, former mayor, Gary Shaw, now a current council member, and I, attended a funeral of one of the victims of the storm. Gary is one of the nicest, most genuine people you will ever meet. I have mentioned that Gary is the administrator for a local large church in Joplin, and fills in for their pastor when necessary. I knew he would be comfortable in the funeral setting given his professional experience and warm demeanor. Gary knew I wanted to pay my respects to not only the victim of the funeral we attended, but all of the victims. We didn't want to detract from the funeral in any way, so we slipped into the church and sat on the very last row. We left immediately after the funeral out of respect for the family. The only indicator of our attendance was our innocuous signatures in the back of the condolence book.

There had been a series of funerals during the first few weeks following May 22nd—all somber reminders that the tornado ripped not only our town apart, but left families without fathers, mothers, sisters, brothers, friends, and neighbors. The city could be rebuilt, but our city's most grievous losses would never be restored.

"Don't Think It Can't Happen To You!"

I rounded out a busy day on the 9th by attending the first meeting of the site selection committee for the new location for St. John's Regional Hospital. Their nine-story building had been devastated by the tornado. Their leaders had graciously invited several city representatives to be on that committee. I wasn't sure of all their reasons for relocating, but I'm sure that one of them was that if the tornado had been 1/4 mile to the south, Joplin would have lost both of the city's hospitals given the proximate location of Freeman Hospital.

On Friday June 10th, we had a meeting with regional Housing and Urban Development officials, as well as some from Washington D.C. We discussed a number of things with a special emphasis on housing. During that meeting we found out the World Trade Center attacks had seen a 3 billion dollar appropriation amendment in Community Development Block

Grant funds to help in recovery efforts; the Katrina flood disaster in Louisiana had received two billion; and the 2008 Midwest floods received an 800 million dollar increase in aid. I filed these numbers away for future reference.

Late that week, I received a blanket email from the International City Management Association (ICMA) advertising a national seminar for city management professionals related to disaster training. I read the resumes of the public managers on the panel who were to provide the training for the seminar. Although any disaster is a horrible thing unto itself, I wondered if any of the situations listed on the program as having been managed by the panel personnel, could be any worse than what I was up against in Joplin. The heading of the email invitation said "Don't Think it Can't Happen to You!" Yielding to temptation, I responded by typing in the words, "I won't" and sent the invitation back from where it came.

Staying Connected to the People

"I couldn't even make out the side of the building. It was total devastation in my view. I just couldn't believe what I saw."

—Kerry Sachetta, Principal
of Joplin High School,
flattened by tornado

At least once a week, following the storm of May 22nd, Fire Chief Randles would take me on a tour of Joplin's storm-damaged area. He would start on Maiden Lane by St. John's Hospital and head east on 26th Street to Main Street, turn north on Main Street and proceed to 20th Street, then straight on to Rangeline Road. This approximate five mile route gave me a snapshot of how the city was progressing and helped me evaluate decisions made in the basement of the Safety Center and those later made from the basement of City Hall. We took another such trip through the Expedited Debris Removal (EDR) area on Monday June 13th stopping along the way to visit with victims. This process, helped to

fulfill Tenet #5 of disaster management: Stay directly connected to the area and people impacted by the disaster.

New Trolley Routes Provided
Transportation for Storm Victims

I had three occasions to visit with a large group of citizens
directly impacted by the storm. The first opportunity came at
the end of the first week when state officials held a meeting at
Missouri Southern University to detail some of the assistance
they could provide. I represented the city at that event and
afterwards intentionally went down into the crowd to speak
to the townspeople directly. I was literally pulled in five different directions at once. Once I explained to those wanting my
attention that I could only have one conversation at a time,
I was able to focus on a lady in her 30's and her mother that
were storm victims. I can't recall the specifics of her question,
but, I do remember it was some issue for which I didn't have
an answer at the moment. I recall telling her, "Just keep reading the city's press releases and we would message an answer
to her question in the near future." I would consistently urge
this during my press conferences and it seemed like it was
working based on the high percentage of citizens that had
responded to direction and registered for help with FEMA.

I learned a valuable lesson that day when she looked at me
and in the nicest, most unassuming way, said, "Mr. Rohr, we
lost everything we had in the tornado. We don't have a house
or a TV or anything else."

I responded by suggesting she buy a copy of the local newspaper, "The Globe" and read the upcoming press releases for

information. She replied, "I don't have a car to get a paper; it was destroyed in the tornado, too!"

I needed to hear that, because I was urging people to do things they were not capable of doing. The tornado had propelled them into living on such a base, elemental level; one which I fully could not understand. The lady's mom stood at her side, quietly listening with tears welling up in her eyes. I felt horrible, but, in that instance I realized we could utilize the city's public transportation system, and more specifically the trolley, to provide basic transportation services for the storm victims.

After working my way through the audience, I went back to the EOC and directed staff to establish new trolley routes into the storm-damaged areas for the foreseeable future and provide rides at no cost. I used other opportunities to speak to and learn the needs of storm victims as the recovery progressed. I found the times spent with storm victims the most informative and rewarding of all. The only problem was that the opportunities to meet with all victims in a large group were limited.

Tracking Storm Statistics Difficult at Times

The death toll reached 153 by the start of that fourth week following the storm. Although unstated, we were realistically past the point of recovering anyone alive from search and recovery. We had started the debris removal progress by now. I have already mentioned that Joplin's tornado of May 22nd, 2011 was now on the record books as resulting in the highest number of deceased caused by a tornado since the National Weather Service began keeping records in 1950.

The growing number of fatalities included those passing away in hospitals from injuries sustained in the storm. We hoped we had experienced the last of those, but didn't know for sure. While we had some luck tracking people's condition early on, as time went on, HIPPA (Health Insurance Portability and Accountability Act) regulations governing the release of patient records prevented us from medical information which would have helped tracking any new developments. In more than one instance, the daily obituary in the newspaper would be our only source of tracking victims and the number of related deaths.

We Needed Signed Permission ... Fast

We had begun hauling debris from curbsides, but were struggling with getting the Right of Entry forms signed and returned; forms that would grant permission of debris removal on private properties. After an initial surge of forms being signed and returned, following their introduction at the Town Hall meeting on June 6th, the pace had slowed considerably. We knew that if we had any hope of meeting our August 7th deadline for completion of EDR process, we had to pick up the pace. Leslie Jones, our Finance Director and I were devoting our full attention to this issue. We tried to determine the reasons why victims were not getting the forms processed for debris removal. Was the message not reaching the right people? Was the information confusing in nature? Perhaps a combination of both?

The fundamental concept of a Right of Entry (ROE) form was an easy one; if you wanted to have the Army Corps' contractors clean debris from your entire lot, then you had to sign the form to allow them the legal right to be on your property. When the insurance component was added concerning the need to reimburse FEMA from your insurance proceeds, the issue got more complicated.

My staff had informed me earlier that the typical structure of insurance policies wasn't helping the matter any. I was told that policies don't typically break down settlement proceeds for each individual aspect of the recovery process. More specifically, the overall settlement doesn't stipulate specifically how much money goes toward debris removal.

The entire week of June 13th was devoted primarily to clarifying issues with the ROE forms. We had moved the deadline for returning the form to Friday, June 17th. This would enable us a few more days to clarify our message. I filmed a video, approximately 20 minutes in length, trying to explain the process. We made the video available on our city website, on YouTube, and to the press. With the help of my assistant, I sent my first Twitter message, urging people to sign the forms. Staff members had been using Facebook since the days following the tornado. I was told we had over 4 million hits on our Facebook account from May 24 to June 17th following the tornado. This exposure, via the internet, undoubtedly played a role in the outpouring of volunteerism we experienced throughout our recovery.

We scheduled an event on Friday June 17th, specifically designed as a last push to get people to turn in their forms. We had some chefs from New Orleans in town, that had been in Joplin for a while providing meals to relief workers. They had agreed to provide Cajun food as an inducement to get people out for the upcoming event.

Early Tuesday morning June 14th, I received a call from Mitch Randles, our fire chief who informed me that we had an industrial building on 4th street that was fully engulfed in flames. I was beginning to dread Mitch's phone calls, as rarely did they begin or end with good news. I got up, showered and dressed quickly, then jumped into my SUV to travel to the site of the fire, which was really close to the Safety Building EOC. Sure enough, it was just as Mitch had described. I saw both the property owner and the tenants of the building there, and spoke to them briefly before traveling the short distance to the EOC. The building would prove to be a total loss, joining the ranks of thousands of others in Joplin with its skeletal remains.

New Trailers Roll into Joplin to Help the Homeless

Just before noon that day, Planning Director, Troy Bolander, picked me up behind City Hall and we went out to see the first manufactured housing unit (trailer) that was placed on a vacant commercial pad at a trailer park just north of Joplin.

Just before we were set to enter the unit, my phone rang and Libby Turner, the lead FEMA manager was on the other end. She was returning my phone call from the previous day. The reason I called Libby was to lobby her to approve the demolition of the remaining structures in the EDR as part of an economic development consideration. Moreover, if these 1,500 partially remaining homes weren't brought down, they would serve as hulking reminders of the tornado and impede rebuilding efforts. It made no sense to me why these structures were not considered part of the debris removal process on FEMA's part.

She was very non-committal in responding to my request. She was in Columbia, Missouri, attending to some flooding issues in the northern part of Missouri. I would learn later that her distance from Joplin that day was metaphor for positions we would both take on the demolition question. FEMA would later decide *not* to fund the demolition portion of the disaster recovery process that I had requested.

Troy and I were pleased with the manufactured housing unit. It was brand new, as they would all be, and it was furnished. Although spartan in appointments, the units would be more than adequate for the 18-month time period for which they would be needed. The most important element was the time frame; it had been only twenty-three days after the tornado and the first manufacturing housing unit was already in the Joplin area at one of the the commercial sites!

FEMA was constantly phoning all the storm victims to gauge housing needs. Based on this information, Troy and I extrapolated that we would need anywhere from 900-1000 units. The guy providing our tour was the FEMA person in charge of the housing operation and he felt we would end up around the 500 level based on his experience and intuition.

Thank God for Caring People

The remainder of the day of June 14th would consist of a series of meetings, including a United Way meeting to review applications from social organizations for funding for victims. An enterprising young man living in Columbia, Missouri, who was originally from Joplin, had started a fund-raising effort there to benefit the city of Joplin and the victims of the tornado. Well over a million dollars had already been raised in a short amount of time and I was one of four board members deciding on how to allocate the funds to 501c (3) organizations that would help those in need. Later that evening, I traveled to the storm-ravaged high school to take part in a fundraiser organized by regional news stations.

Staff Needed and Deserved Some Rest

I had reduced my hours to an 85-hour work week and was rotating department heads out of the schedule to provide each with some well-deserved rest. The continuous demand for our time and attention was starting to take a toll on our already very thin staff. City employees had done a wonderful job to date, but the stress was starting to show; some of our staff had lost their own homes which added to the pressure they felt daily.

The net effect was that I had to be flexible to accommodate certain personal situations and I needed to get them out of the EOC for a time, so they could return with renewed focus and energy. The result was that those of us at the helm would have to take on more of the load.

Breaking Down the Debris Removal Process

Late Wednesday afternoon, June 15th, I met with Rob O'Brian, President of the Joplin Chamber of Commerce, and Troy Bolander, at my office to discuss a list of names to serve on the Citizens Advisory Recovery Team (*CART)* committee. This was a citizen-based planning committee organized to discuss plans to rebuild a third of our city. We selected a list of 20 or so names in the community that we felt represented a cross-section of the community. We didn't have time to utilize normal procedures for establishing a committee, as we knew that process would create a lag time of months before the group would produce its recommendations for rebuilding. We had to get started. I thought it was important to email this list to Mayor Woolston for his review and I did just that.

That following Friday, we thought it would be helpful to demonstrate to the press and in turn the public, the full scope of the property debris removal process. So we held a press event at a site in the relative center of the storm area. A Corps' contractor chose a heavily damaged lot and began working on removing the mounds of debris. Participants then returned to the same site four hours later to view the same lot, now completely cleared. I attended both ends of the event and spent time after the 1:00 p.m. initial portion, making myself available to the press for interview. The live demonstration proved to be very effective and encouraging.

Brief Encounter Brings Report of a True Miracle

At six o'clock, that same evening, we started to see the first of hundreds of people that flooded City Hall for the Right of Entry event spoken of earlier. Originally scheduled to occur in the parking lot, we had moved it indoors, as the entire Midwest section of the country was experiencing a series of 100 plus degree days that would plague us the entire summer. The chefs from New Orleans had come through for us and the gumbo and jambalaya was flowing. Leslie Jones, David Hertzberg, the Public Works Director, and I were perched at a table on the first floor lobby area trying to answer questions in an effort to get more forms signed.

After a while, I left the group and made my way to the area serving the great smelling food. I got my plate and went to sit on the floor to eat my dinner, a short distance away from the main tables. I saw a man seated at a nearby table who was eyeballing me. I didn't think too much of it, because I had been on television frequently in recent days and folks were beginning to recognize me, especially Joplin residents. After I finished eating, the man sauntered over and squatted down next to me and said, "You were at the church that night, weren't you?"

It suddenly dawned on me why he had looked familiar. I responded quickly, "Yes, I was there!"

He introduced himself as Fred, and then added, "I was there, too, helping pull people out of that mess."

I felt an immediate bond with Fred from that shared experience. We talked about that horrible night of May 22nd and he shared with me that his house, which had been situated near the flattened church, was destroyed also. He and his girlfriend had ridden out the storm while huddled in the bathtub and then, they selflessly made their way over to the church to help rescue the people trapped in the debris.

After a while, Fred looked at me and said, "You know that lady who you lifted out of the pile?"

"Yes, I remember," I said, shaking my head, thinking, *how can I forget?*

Suddenly Fred interjected, "She's alive!"

I was stunned and nearly fell over from my sitting position. Fred continued, "After you set her down, my girlfriend went up to her and pounded her chest a few times. The woman coughed and vomited onto her and started breathing!"

I thought surely he must be confused, but, Fred called his girlfriend over from the table and she corroborated his story. I couldn't wait to call Mitch and tell him. I have tried many times to describe how I felt after hearing Fred's news. There was disbelief at first, then relief, then total awe. I was immensely grateful that God spared me one less nightmarish memory of that tragic night. Instead I had a reason to rejoice.

Looks Like Bombing in Kuwait

The following day was a Saturday and I had a meeting with a local contractor and a representative from Phillips and Jordan, Inc., the primary Army Corps' contractor, who had efficiently handled the first portion of the debris removal contract. I knew the firm was interested in the second phase of the contract, which was being bid out as we spoke. I was careful, as were they, not to cross any lines in the discussion because of their pending bid. The interesting thing about this meeting, from my standpoint, was an observation made by the representative from Phillips and Jordan, Inc., a guy named Allen Morse. He was a seasoned veteran of 37 years with extensive experience in cleaning up war zones and the results of natural disasters.

Allen struck me as a serious professional; someone not prone to frivolous chatter or arbitrary observations. He honestly appraised the damage, "What happened in Joplin is as bad as I have seen in my career, in terms of overall damage. The only thing I can compare it to, is damage rendered by a 'carpet bomb' in Kuwait."

My Children Needed Me, Too

I had made a decision earlier in the week of June 13th that I wasn't fully comfortable with. After repeated questions about when the EOC would move back to City Hall, I decided we would do so for the start of business on Thursday June 23rd. I had misgivings about doing so, fearful that we would lose the sense of immediacy that was still required by the emergency response efforts. Realistically, however, the safety services aspect to the storm had ended. It was time to become fully engaged in the debris removal phase.

I also had second thoughts about taking the upcoming Father's Day off. It was Father's Day, 2011. During the twenty-eight days since the storm, I had largely ignored my family, working nearly non-stop. I was remorseful about not spending time with them, but, also felt guilty about taking a day off when so much was still to be accomplished. I felt the pull of fifty thousand people who were depending on me, but, I knew my wife and children needed me, too. They needed a Father's Day more than me.

Telling Joplin's Story

> "The human spirit is designed to rise to a challenge and meet it head-on. The human spirit is itself a miracle …"
>
> —Ronda Del Boccio, Best Selling Author
> Write on Purpose.com

The sixth week following the tornado started out on a positive note. FEMA had responded to my urgings by continuing to order Mobile Housing units (MHU's) on an ongoing basis. Two hundred more were ordered, giving us a total of four hundred and sixty units, either in Joplin at a nearby site being inspected, or en route. I had heard there were some problems with people being exposed to formaldehyde from some of the trailers during the Katrina flooding disaster, so there were inspections of the units at the staging area, prior to actually placing them. I still didn't know exactly how many units we would need, but, I was pleased that the process was working.

Where'd You Go, Joe?

Vice-President Biden had been scheduled for a visit that week. I had been notified of the pending visit by a FEMA representative and had worked with the police department to plan the logistics. I commented to staff that the Vice President and the Pope were the only two dignitaries that *hadn't* visited Joplin, yet. (I was raised in the Catholic faith, so felt comfortable with the humorous observation). For some unknown reason, Biden cancelled his visit at the last minute.

Nuisance Abatement—Necessary to Clean-Up

I was starting to meet with selected department heads relative to the nuisance abatement process. It had become apparent that we were going to have a significant number of properties that would not be cleaned by private insurance or with the help of the contractors from the Army Corps through the right of entry forms. We didn't know all the circumstances surrounding these properties, although we suspected some owners had abandoned the property and just left town. We had to give these property owners a deadline then, if no response was received, the city could have the work done ourselves through what is known as a nuisance abatement process. If the city was forced to handle things in this manner, we could place a lien on the property and recover our money when the property was eventually sold. This issue and the moratorium would be discussed at our first post storm, regularly-scheduled council meeting to be held in June.

Home Depot Back in Business

Earlier in the day, some council members and I attended a store reopening ceremony at the temporary Home Depot store on Rangeline Road. Home Depot had constructed this temporary facility, in short order, out of a canvas type material. It looked like a huge white tent. They would use this temporary set up, while rebuilding their store on the same location as the original one. The symbolism and practicality of the reopening was significant. Joplin's main source of revenue was the sales tax and we couldn't receive sales tax unless the stores were open.

Making Progress

Early the following day, we went on another tour of the Expedited Debris Removal (EDR) area. I was insistent that we travel the same route, so I could compare what I saw directly with the mental picture I retained based on the maps we were reviewing. Although the storm debris was still staggering, I was pleased to see that we were making progress. We had several hundred trash-hauling trucks active at this point.

Late in the afternoon of June 21st, I attended a long term recovery meeting at the Chamber. This was a group of prominent business leaders in the community that apparently had convened prior to this meeting, to discuss the direction for Joplin in the future. Genuine concern lined the faces of everyone at the table in the Chamber's largest meeting room. I presented a report which included a progress update, detailing each step in the disaster recovery process. Following the meeting, Chamber President, Rob O'Brian, thanked me for attending.

My comments had provided an outline by which further discussion could take place. I felt good about that. I know these were the leaders of Joplin and they could convey the message to others that things were under control and moving forward. The function of this group would later morph into the mission of the CART oversight board.

Overwhelming Work Impacted Communication

There had been an unintended breakdown of communication regarding the responsibilities and jurisdictions in the community. I had assumed the lead role in dealing with the 7,500 homes impacted and the residents that had lived in those structures. Rob O'Brian, Joplin's Chamber of Commerce Director and leading economic development director for the city, spearheaded the effort to provide help to the 500 or so businesses impacted, then CJ Huff, Joplin's School Superintendent, led the R-8's effort to reopen schools on time later in the summer, despite extensive damage to many of their buildings. Although the communication between the three entities was active at the start, it diminished over time, as we all became immersed in our individual challenges and responsibilities.

Debris Removal Was a Constant Challenge

Early Wednesday morning on June 22nd, I met with Leslie Jones, the Finance Director and Jack Schaller, Assistant Public Works Director, to discuss the debris removal progress. They were jointly handling the specifics of the daily activities on debris removal. By this time, we were receiving updated maps from the Public Works Department that served as the basis for our talks. Daily reports from the Army Corps, along with in-field inspections by the staff of the Public Works Department, went to our Geographic Information Systems (*GIS*) mapping division, which in turn made changes in the daily map updates we received and noted on the maps displayed on tables in the basement at City Hall.

Once a week, we would meet and discuss progress we saw on the maps through our in-field inspections. In this manner, we made decisions and managed the removal of remaining mountains of debris.

"… in the City," I Suggested

At lunchtime on June 22nd, we had our second meeting with St. John's hospital officials to discuss their new location. The hospital had been destroyed by the tornado. Our first meeting was held in a meeting room at a local hotel, but proved to be a loud and noisy setting, so I offered to let them use City Hall, which they accepted. I was pleased to hear of the sites they were considering. Two were in the city, and the third could be easily annexed into Joplin. I hadn't really been joking, but there were laughs at the previous meeting when they asked me what characteristics I thought the new site ought to have. My response was that it had to have one characteristic, "That it be in the city," I said, and I meant it. Joplin couldn't accept St. John's Hospital being located outside our corporate boundaries. We needed their service and presence in our community.

Meeting Budget Deadline

Just before a meeting with Leslie Jones to discuss next year's budget, I learned the storm's death toll had risen to 156. I hoped this would be our final number, but knew there was a good chance there would be additional victims. Despite this grim update, we had to make some decisions about the pending budget which had to be approved and in place by November 1st. Given the fact that the two of us typically spent more time on the budget than anyone else, and that we were totally immersed in disaster recovery, I decided we would utilize an abridged budget, using the same line items from the current year's budget in most every instance. There really was not another choice.

One Hundred and Twenty-Two Messages and Counting

Thursday, June 23rd marked the Emergency Operations Center (EOC) *move* from the Safety Center to City Hall. It felt a little strange to see the offices again; I had only been in the building a handful of times since May 22nd. I remember one of those instances, when I returned to the building late in the day during the third week following the storm. I had left the Safety Center at about 6:30 p.m. wanting to get home at a reasonable hour. I stopped by City Hall to check on a few things and when I entered my office on the second floor I saw the red light blinking on my phone reflecting unheard messages. After listening to the one hundred and twenty-two messages later, I decided to call it a night.

I had made provisions for my calls to be transferred to another office, but obviously it wasn't working. I listened to calls that came in from all over the country; from mother's wanting to know where to send a check with the proceeds from their daughter's lemonade stand to local government entities wanting to send money from their General Fund, and most everything in between. I was genuinely moved by the outpouring of love and support contained in these messages. I retuned the next day to listen to forty-five additional messages, similar to those from the day before.

We Could Rebuild Faster by Waiting

There was a special city council meeting held on the evening of Thursday, June 23rd. The purpose of the meeting was for the council to make a determination on whether to improve standards concerning residential construction in the EDR area and to decide on whether to implement a residential building moratorium. Passions were running high, as many citizens wanted to begin reconstruction of their homes as soon as possible, in order to regain some sense of normalcy in their lives. This was understandable, but staff was recommending a pause in residential rebuilding, but not repairs, so that we could achieve our deadline for debris removal of August 7th.

I waited for the most opportune time to make comments in this regard. I cited five reasons, for which I thought the moratorium was necessary, starting with safety concerns:

1. Traffic was bad now, with all the sightseers and contractors coming into town. We expected as many as 600 debris-hauling units to compound this already existing traffic problem, which would require lane closings for an extended period of time. We didn't need construction areas in the middle of all this. It was a bad mix and I stated, "We don't need anyone else in Joplin getting hurt or worse."

2. The second reason to wait for construction activity was because of health considerations. "Even if your home was rebuilt, it is unhealthy to be located next to a big pile of rubble with a distinct possibility of insects and rodents being present," I offered. Although I didn't want to mention it unless I absolutely had to, I had asked the city's Health Director, Dan Pekarek, on May 27th how long

a period before we would have problems with rats. His answer was that it would take two gestation periods, or approximately two months. I had kept that date of July 27th in the back of my mind, as a date on which a bad situation could get even worse. This was an observation I didn't want to bring up specifically at the meeting unless I had to; I didn't think citizens needed to be worried about one more thing. It just made sense to remove all debris before construction projects were underway.

3. The third reason I gave for delaying construction, was timeliness, and the potential impact on the city's budgeting if the debris removal deadline was not met. At that time, we were under the impression that after August 7th, all removal costs would be our responsibility. Jack Schaller and I had done the math on that before the meeting and it came to three million dollars a day. Our reserves wouldn't last long at that rate.

4. The final two reasons I provided to justify a waiting period on residential construction in the EDR, was that it would allow the CART planning process to make significant progress;

5. And also give us a chance to develop some of the incentives and programs we were researching to help with rebuilding efforts.

I concluded my remarks by stating we could build back faster by delaying. I hoped that made sense to everyone. I recommended that we narrow the moratorium to 60 days and than we would re-open areas in the city as cleanup progress dictated. After more discussion, council passed the measure by a 7-2 vote.

I recall that our typically reserved Mayor, Mike Woolston, ended that meeting on an emotional note; thanking the city staff and those who had volunteered time and money to help Joplin. By the time he finished, many in the room were in tears, including the guy seated directly to his left behind the city manager's name plate.

How Do We Tell This Story?

On Friday, June 24th I had a very interesting meeting in the basement of City Hall with the Director of Joplin's museum, Brad Belk, local businessman Doug Hunt, and Pat Tuttle, the Director of Joplin's Convention and Visitors Bureau. The purpose of the meeting was to talk about eventual possibilities to tastefully and respectfully tell the story of the tornado, at the appropriate time in the future.

I had asked Pat to save the semi-truck that was wrapped around a tree on the northeast end of the St. John's hospital property. I thought, what better way to show someone that wasn't here on May 22nd, the force of nature unleashed on Joplin by saving and displaying that ribbon of metal that once was a semi-truck? Mother Nature had literally tied the truck around a tree that day. I think all four of us realized that Joplin was, and continued to be, the focus of nationwide attention and the city would be defined not only by what had happened that day, but also for how we responded to the disaster. We thought that paying respect to those citizens we lost and tastefully recounting the story would be important to Joplin and our future and also help other communities at the same time.

The discussion led to the thought that the tree and the truck could be the focal point to a museum telling the story of the storm and that the outer portion of the courtyard for the museum building could be a metaphor for the aftermath of the storm and "The Miracle of the Human Spirit" that was occurring in our city. We didn't know how exactly to tell the story, but it was a birth of a concept that could demonstrate to all that something good could come out of something bad.

We had started to call attention to the incredible support we were receiving by providing all of volunteers and people assisting us with blue wristbands which included the words, "Miracle of the Human Spirit–Joplin MO 2011." There was also a variety of Joplin t-shirts that were becoming available with reassuring and reaffirming messages.

State of Recovery Update

Later that day, we held a "State of the Recovery" press conference. We had not had a press conference in a while and though it was time to provide an update on our efforts as a whole. Since we had moved back to City Hall, we changed the location of the conferences to the second floor lobby area. I was surrounded by department heads to help me answer specific questions following my initial statement. I hadn't made any pretense throughout all of the press conferences that I had all the answers, because I *didn't.* I started all the conferences off with a statement, and then opened the meeting up for any questions from reporters. If I could answer the questions I did. If not, I would step aside and let the appropriate department head respond. At this particular conference I relayed that we were about 50% done with the debris removal process. I also informed them that we had lost another citizen, who had died of natural causes at one of our few remaining shelters. The fatality count stood at 158 on that day.

The press conferences were indicative of the Tenet #6 of disaster management that I had learned from our experiences: Designate one spokesperson to provide accurate accounts of progress; one who will reassure the public regarding the future.

I had people tell me after the initial few weeks of chaos, they found my appearance both calming and reassuring during the crisis. I am grateful for that affirmation. I'm not sure whether it was my natural monotone, which has put many a listener to sleep over the years, or hopefully, they had come to rely on my updates that provided them with some specific information, especially during those first hectic weeks. I also was surprised at how simple phrases I uttered at press conferences were being reused and restated in different instances throughout Joplin. It helped me realize what a powerful tool those press conferences were and the importance of always choosing my words wisely.

Photo Section Pages

Looking West at the wreckage with the 9-story high St. John's Hospital on the horizon

First responders deploy in Joplin after the tornado

Looking Southeast from Maiden Lane

*Remnants of the semi-truck wrapped around a
tree directly off of 26th street in Joplin*

*In the foreground the remnants of the life flight
helicopter used by St. John's Hospital*

*President Obama surrounded by Joplin city staff. Taken on
May 29th, 2011 just west of the former Joplin High School*

Cars were tossed around throughout the storm damage area

First responders navigating through Joplin's
Main Street area following the tornado

The only thing left standing in this scene is
the Missouri American water tower

The remants of the Academy sporting goods store on Rangeline Road

More devastation in Joplin. Long time residents lost
their bearings as most everything in sight was gone

This shot depicts damage at a strip mall on Rangeline Road.

Debris caught by one of the few trees left standing in the storm area

*Joplin had two fire stations destroyed on May 22, 2011.
Below are the remants of one of those buildings.*

Looking South towards St. John's Hospital along Maiden Lane.

This photo reflects destruction at a destroyed
Joplin School on 26th Street

St. John's Hospital looking North

*Another photo showing St. John's Hospital. Notice
all the windows have been blown out.*

A destroyed home in Joplin

Cloud cover over a storm-ravaged Joplin

*Sheer and utter devastation where homes and
buildings once covered the landscape*

A car marked for removal West of the Wal-Mart parking lot with the battered Academy sporting goods building in the background

One of the few remaining homes in the expedited debris removal (EDR) area

Flag flies at half mast in front of Joplin High School

One corner of a house left standing after the tornado

*Message to loved ones and relatives on a storm
shelter whose occupants survived the tornado*

One of the few remaining traffic signs left standing

Another view of the devastation

*First responders weave their way through
the western section of Joplin*

Those Who Came and Those Who Gave

"For it is more blessed to give, than to receive ..."

—Acts 20:35; King James Bible

As stated in previous chapter, something very unique started to evidence itself in the moments following the tornado that had done nothing but grow in the days, weeks and months since May 22nd. It was something that was as apparent to me as the battered asphalt I stood on in the Cunningham Park parking lot on May 29th, when I first used the term "The Miracle of the Human Spirit." The phrase had caught on and heard it repeated again and again following the one week observance event on the 29th. I don't know that I am smart enough to explain the reasons for "the miracle" but, I am a witness to its manifestations.

The "Show Me State"

Being a native of Ohio, I was surprised at how conservative Joplin was when I arrived in 2004. I considered myself conservative, but soon realized I didn't know the meaning of the word in comparison. One of the ways I came to that understanding was by mishandling an issue early on after my arrival as the new city manager. I learned from that mistake and others that there was very little nuance in making judgments in Joplin. Rather, I had to make judgments "by the book", so to speak, based on facts alone. I also learned how this conservative nature is part and parcel of the reputation for Missouri as the "Show Me State."

The residents of Joplin didn't waste a lot of time worrying about things that weren't visible needs. Missourians' approach to life is very practical and certain secondary things just aren't important. For someone who had spent a lot of time thinking about how things should be, I realized that I had a challenge ahead of me. To be successful in my leadership position I had to understand where I was and have an appreciation for those I would serve. My experiences with the citizens of Joplin in the aftermath of the tornado, has led me to a deeper appreciation of their conservative values.

"The Miracle," Demonstrated

In the time directly after the tornado, I saw countless examples of neighbors helping neighbors. Many selflessly ignored their own losses to help locate and free men, women, and children from the debris all around. Some transported those in need of medical attention in the beds of their own pick up trucks. Joplin residents put their own needs aside to care for neighbors, friends, and complete strangers. Many volunteers and responders coming in to Joplin were amazed at the unselfish attitude of residents who had lost everything. Some victims would direct those rending aid and assistance down the street to a neighbor's residence rather than receiving treatment themselves.

Joplin's citizens demonstrated ingrained values of hard work and self reliance to overcome adversity in the aftermath of May 22nd and those values served the city well going forward. Mother Nature may have taken their material possessions, but did nothing but galvanize our spirits in doing so.

These values and beliefs are steeped in a strong faith and helped Joplin through good times and bad. They had also provided the foundation on which the second aspect of "The Miracle of the Human Spirit" was built. I am referring to the incredible outpouring of aid, assistance and overall support we have received throughout the area, state, country, and beyond.

I am not sure I can completely explain the phenomenon. I am sure the magnitude of the loss; losing nearly a third of your city and resultant sympathy had a good deal to do with it. I was too busy to watch most, but caught a couple of segments of the national news covering our plight in the weeks following May 22nd. However, if the number of reporters on the Monday after the storm shading both sides of 26th Street by St. John's Hospital and Cunningham Park was any indication, our story was being told.

It was interesting to note that every visitor, even those who had followed the extensive news coverage, had the exact response after seeing the devastation in person. They would comment that the pictures, videos and news accounts didn't come close to describing the level of destruction they saw in person. It was unfathomable.

There were an estimated 5,000 first responders that rushed to Joplin in the aftermath of the storm. Some arrived, prompted by the news accounts; others came in response to our calls for help and mutual aid arrangements. Others came, guided by a basic, genuine Christian belief that it was the right thing to do. These first responders included police and fire personnel, public works crews, National Guard personnel, FEMA officials, AmeriCorps volunteers, and ordinary people from throughout the region, state and country. There is no question that together, they saved lives and performed the initial work in difficult circumstances to set the stage for future successes. They were all part of "The Miracle of the Human Spirit." I wish I could thank them all personally for such sacrifices of time, energy, and love.

To date, Joplin has seen 95,000 registered volunteers come to town to assist in the primary function of debris removal and lot cleanup, as well as many other helpful initiatives. In addition, there was a large percentage of that original number of unregistered volunteers that went directly into the field to provide assistance. They have braved incredible circumstances to do so. We had a protracted period of approximately a month soon following the tornado, where temperatures exceeded a hundred degrees, with a high of 110 degrees during that period, yet they came. They came in church groups, civic organization, groups from cities, families and individuals all wanting to help Joplin. They, too, are part of "The Miracle of the Human Spirit."

Lord, Forgive Me

The city of Joplin, the Joplin R-8 school system and other entities in the city have received financial donations from literally throughout the world to assist in our recovery efforts. I recall CJ Huff, the school superintendent, holding up a dollar bill at an earlier press conference and telling the story a child outside of Joplin dipping into their piggy bank to send a solitary dollar to help in the school's rebuilding efforts. There was a story of a mother in Texas, whose daughter had organized friends to raise money to buy stuffed animals for kids in Joplin who had lost all their toys. I recalled a letter from a lady in Illinois and an accompanying check for $1,000 sent to my attention, based on her seeing a snippet of me at one of the press conferences. That same day, we received a letter with a $50 bill in it from a guy from New York State. These people didn't even know us, but were sending help. I cried when I opened these two letters that caused me to reflect on my life and recall specific times when I had been self absorbed or uncaring. I had a lot to learn and I was learning it from those that were part of "The Miracle of the Human Spirit." We also received a quilt from a lady in Arizona and blankets from a woman in my home state of Ohio.

We Heard From Celebrities

Joplin received donations from celebrities that were better positioned financially to help. Sheryl Crow, a Missouri native, graciously donated her prized 1959 Rolls to be auctioned off to benefit the school system. Rush Limbaugh brought a $100,000 check to the city on a visit that he made to our July 4th celebration and Brad Pitt and Angelina Jolie donated $500,000 from their Make It Right foundation. It is my understanding that Brad grew up in nearby Springfield, Missouri. From the child that donated the dollar, to the celebrity contributions, all were part of "The Miracle of the Human Spirit."

As I stated previously, providing quick intermediate housing options and minimizing population loss were immediate priorities of the City of Joplin. The warm nature of our citizenry came through immediately as people opened their homes up to friends and relatives who were displaced. 7,500 homes were impacted by the storm, with nearly half of these homes being destroyed or uninhabitable. We quickly set up shelters to augment the efforts of private individuals taking people into their homes.

We also began urging people to register with FEMA, for assistance with housing, which they did in large numbers. Many people were provided resources to be housed in commercial rental units as a result of this funding.

Lastly, as mentioned, we strongly encouraged FEMA to get the manufactured housing units on site as soon as possible. Short term, we were able to provide housing means to those in need. It is too early to tell the long-term effect of these efforts. But if the school systems returning students percentage of more than 95% of last year's students is any indication, Joplin has showed very well in terms of minimizing population loss. These collective housing efforts were part of "The Miracle of the Human Spirit."

The local school system was especially hard hit by the tornado suffering in excess of 150 million dollars in damage to ten buildings, four of which were completely destroyed. Early on their leaders, including CJ Huff, the Superintendent of Schools, determined they would retrofit existing buildings in the community, for use as temporary school facilities in an attempt to open schools on time by August 17th. This effort included the conversion of a vacant building at the local mall to be used by the 11th and 12th grade students; one of those students would be my stepson.

Through the tireless efforts of school officials, local architects and contractors (among others), schools opened on time, restoring a semblance of routine and normalcy to the scrambled lives of both students and their parents. This was yet another example of "The Miracle of the Human Spirit."

Pets Also Affected by Storm's Violence

Some of the forgotten victims of the tornado were household pets, who lost their homes and, in some instances, their masters on May 22nd. I recall riding with Fire Chief, Mitch Randles and Health Director, Dan Pekarek, late on the evening of Monday, May 23rd. We were driving west on 26th Street when we spotted the spectral image of an all-white dog, a Husky, traipsing through the debris. It was dark and more than a little eerie as we observed the dog sniffing the ground and shattered remains of a home. I felt for the solitary dog and wondered what had happened to its owners and where it was headed in this vast horizon of nothingness.

I asked Mitch to stop his vehicle, then climbed out and tried to hail the dog, but, the closer I got to him the faster he moved off into the dark. I had hopes we could take him to the Humane Society on North Main Street where he could possibly be reunited with his owner. Fortunately, we had better luck in helping pets in the weeks following the storm than I had that night.

Aided by the Health Department under Dan's leadership, the City partnered with the Humane Society to reunite nearly 500 lost pets with their owners. Being a pet owner myself, I recognized the value of pets to a family and felt good about helping animals get back to the families that loved them.

Unfortunately, following the storm, many additional animals become available at the Humane Society. On Saturday and Sunday June 25th and 26th, an adoption event was held for the 745 animals on hand. People came from several states to rescue these animals. All 745 found new homes! Another example of "The Miracle of the Human Spirit."

Debris Removal Also a "Miracle"

To attempt to describe the destruction and amount of debris that lay in the Expedited Debris Removal (EDR) area in mere words would be an effort in futility. To repeat, pictures proved inadequate in comparison as verified by each and every visitor who saw the results of the tornado in person. There was sheer and utter destruction as wide and as far as one could see.

A well kept house was now a pile of rubble in thousands of broken pieces. Family's possessions were strewn about in chest-deep rubble. The trees that remained standing had no branches or bark. Thousands of cars were tossed randomly along the six mile long and nearly one mile wide storm path, many twisted and contorted in ways reminiscent of the damage sustained in the worst head-on collisions.

City officials, along with the Army Corps of Engineers estimated a total of 300 million cubic yards of debris resulting from the tornado. Thinking of where to start was intimidating, let alone envisioning completion of the task in 68 days.

But finish it we did. We did it through a group effort involving the citizens of Joplin, an incredible number of volunteers, FEMA, the Army Corps of Engineers and their contractors, the National Guard and city employees. We did it because we sublimated egos, demonstrated mental toughness and were incredibly organized. It wasn't perfect, but the transformation of Joplin in a short amount of time was incredible. This too was an example of "The Miracle of the Human Spirit."

Warehouses Full of "Miracles"

One day a group of volunteers, along with some city employees, made me aware of a significant part of the assistance effort going on that I needed to see. It was five weeks or so after the tornado and I had spent a good deal of time in the office overseeing the entirety of the storm recovery efforts. So, in response to their requests, we scheduled a field trip to visit the warehouses nearby to see all of the items being donated to help storm victims.

Our first stop was a warehouse off Main Street on the north end of the Joplin. I walked into a huge structure that was totally full of household items from diapers to bug spray and everything in between. There were swarms of teenage volunteers sorting items for distribution. Fork lifts were removing skids from storage racks to bring to the sorters. Orders were being filled by the dock doors with trucks waiting to take the items to churches, where they would be distributed to those in need. Their efforts were organized, professional and efficient.

We then visited a food bank in nearby Springfield, Missouri; a building which also had a large cooler and freezer.

I was told there were two other similar warehouses nearby and that approximately 2/3 of the food in all three buildings was destined for daily deliveries to Joplin.

Our next stop was Marshfield, Missouri, where an old warehouse had been set up to receive every clothing item you could think of. There had to be enough clothes for the next three generations of family members of those impacted by the tornado. The group that was giving me the tour also informed me there was bottled water stored in Carthage, Missouri and more clothes and water being collected in Neosho, Missouri. I was stunned by the extensive donation system and amount of materials contributed to the relief effort. The donated items represented thousands of people with caring hearts, who became part of "The Miracle of the Human Spirit."

—

July 4th—Proud to be Americans

"You here from Joplin, Missouri are the essence of what the founding fathers had in mind. You are the epitome of what makes this country work. Joplin will be rebuilt to be greater than before and you will show the country how it's done."

—Rush Limbaugh,
Author and Conservative Talk Show Host
July 4, 2011

At the start of the sixth week following the May 22nd tornado that shook Joplin, Missouri to its core, we initiated CEO meetings to be held on each Monday. Besides me, present at these meetings would be lead FEMA representative, Mike Karl, the leader of the Army Corps of Engineers, Colonel Patton, and Colonel Ward of the Missouri National Guard. It was a good idea to meet regularly because I had opportunity to call attention to any problems, or potential problems observed, and the other three men could quickly address them.

During one of the meetings, the only thing I could think of was to express concern about the consistency and numbers production of the new contractor for the Army Corps. I felt that if we didn't get a handle on it, we might not make our deadline. Colonel Patton would give me a projected number, in terms of yards cleared per day early on, but stopped doing so when I remembered those numbers and reminded him at subsequent meetings that we weren't hitting those targets. It wasn't that he was not conscientious; rather it was problems with the transition of the contractors. The new contractor was having some trouble learning the routine.

The afternoon of Monday, June 27th, I was scheduled to appear before a Missouri House Committee that was convening at Webster Hall on the campus of Missouri Southern State University. I spent time Monday, late morning and afternoon, fine-tuning some numbers on storm damage and on the response in an attempt to be as accurate as possible at the hearing. I was the first to speak, in what appeared to me to be a fairly crowded auditorium. I didn't really have a point to drive home, so I focused my testimony on conveying our overview of the response. The legislators seemed like a receptive audience. Figuring they could be in a position to help, I did make the point of the need to designate certain proceeds in an insurance settlement to a specific function. Several of them scribbled notes, when I made that statement, and I hoped something useful would come from it.

False Alarm Gratefully

On Wednesday June 29th, I received an alarming call while in the basement of City Hall. A spotter at one of the landfills had seen what they thought was a human rib cage. I immediately let the police and fire departments know of this and they dispatched teams to investigate. Fire Chief Randles and I had both stated early on that we would both be surprised if there were *no* such discoveries given the vastness and depth of the debris field. This prediction was made despite the missing persons list being cleared. We both hoped we'd be wrong. Perhaps this grim prophecy was coming true? I was careful not to overreact, so I stayed at my desk in the basement. I was relieved about an hour later when I received a report from the police department that the discovery was a Halloween prop that had been mistaken for something else.

Many Victims Still in Hospital

I am not sure about the anecdotal of the information, but I was given an estimate around this time, that there were still about 90 victims of the tornado in hospitals. We knew these survivors were in hospitals spread out over three states but, had no idea on how they were doing. The number of fatalities had reached 158 and we prayed those 90 would completely recover and not be added to that statistic.

"Wheel of Fortune" Game Show Scouting Joplin for a Segment

The week of the 29th of June was like every week after the tornado, in that it saw several groups come forward with programs to help Joplin. These groups ranged from green energy interests on construction properties to a Wheel of Fortune advance team scouting out a location for a segment to focus attention on Joplin. These groups, programs and events also contributed to "The Miracle of the Human Spirit," being demonstrated everyday.

Important Visitor from FEMA

Thursday June 30th saw the first meeting of the CART group take place at the Chamber of Commerce building. FEMA had been careful to describe the input process as citizen-driven, so all of us from the City who were experienced in working with a group like this attended the meeting, but shied away from taking control. As a result, the first meetings of the CART group were limited in terms of accomplishments but, the effort gained traction once leadership was established. Even in these early meetings, the CART membership knew it would need to hold public meetings to gain valuable citizen input and they also started discussing ways to stage these meetings.

On Friday the first of July, I received an interesting visit from someone described to me as the number three person at FEMA, Bill Carwile, Associate Administrator for Response and Recovery. Bill was accompanied by Mike Karl, the FEMA field representative who took charge of Joplin efforts when Libby Turner relocated. I received Bill and Mike in my office area in the basement of City Hall, which consisted of two partial dividers, four chairs including the one I sat in, two folding tables, a computer and a phone.

Bill is an older gentleman with a wealth of real world experience. I was very interested in FEMA's culture and how they operated, based on news accounts with respect to some of their earlier efforts. He was very complimentary of Joplin's efforts to date and especially noted the speed in which the streets were cleared. Bill went on to say, "We are only as good as local leadership enables us to be."

I understood very clearly, what he meant. My conversation with Bill and my, evolving experience, leads to Tenet #7 of disaster management: Local leadership is the essential ingredient in disaster response. Don't wait for FEMA to tell you what to do. The local jurisdiction needs to take control and direct others to help accordingly. FEMA and other groups that arrive on site, work for you in your jurisdiction and not the other way around. Be prepared for the faces of FEMA reps to change a lot through the course of the disaster. Ask them for a hierarchal chart of their employees present in your community and request they update this on an on-going basis. This will help you determine who is whose boss and who reports to whom. Also, ask for a condensed chart of services they can provide for your community. You won't have the time or temperament to read a lengthy prepared publication.

A New Hospital and Rebuilding Businesses a Priority

Later in the day, certain members of city staff toured the sites proposed for St. John's Hospital. The others in the group probably had a better feel for the proposed locations then I did, so the trip probably helped me visualize the potential more than the others. The site chosen for the new hospital location was critical because it would have a long-term impact on the city. I liked the 50th and Main Street alternative on the city's southern border before the visit and liked it even more after seeing the other proposed sites.

Later that day, July 1st, we met with representatives from the Chamber of Commerce, who had taken the lead to investigate individual company's plans for both debris removal and reconstruction for businesses impacted by the tornado. I was pleased those initial contacts had yielded positive results. Chamber officials were optimistic about both the progress of both the debris removal and rebuilding aspects of the commercial sector of Joplin.

July 4th Came and Went

The upcoming July 4th weekend was slated to be a busy one in Joplin. I had always been amazed at the patriotic fervor unleashed in Joplin over the July 4th holiday through the organized parades and fireworks displays, but also in the form of individual and family fireworks being set off seemingly throughout the city. Our family also celebrated my step-son's birthday that weekend. Miles turned 12.

For understandable reasons, the mood and frequency of the fireworks discharging seemed subdued that July. However, there were still many events to attend over the course of the weekend. We had a celebration to honor volunteers at Cunningham Park on Saturday July 2nd. Despite the free food and entertainment, attendance was lower than expected due to the 105 degree temperature that afternoon. The following day, some of the city staff attended a Steve Miller band concert at the nearby Downstream Casino. Joplin's school mascot is an eagle and I was touched when Miller dedicated to Joplin his trademark song, "Fly like an Eagle." I first heard the song, thirty years before in a dorm room when I was a student at Miami University in Oxford, Ohio. There was no way of knowing then, how significant the song would one day be for me.

Rush Limbaugh Helped Us Celebrate!

Finally on the 4th, conservative radio host, Rush Limbaugh came to town to join our holiday celebration festival at Landreth Park. He was touting his new tea line while in town and spent time talking with Mayor Woolston about the city's needs. Rush left a $100,000 check with the Mayor earmarked for the First Response Fund to benefit of the City of Joplin. Many may not be aware of this donation that helped so many.

Four Stages of Disaster Recovery

"It takes many agencies, government and private, as well as many individuals, to help a community and its citizens recover from a disaster. Missourians have demonstrated from day one that they are ready to do whatever it takes to help one another not only survive the Joplin tornado but to thrive over the long run."

—Libby Turner, FEMA News Release,
July 22, 2011

I had never really given much thought to the four stages of disaster recovery until thrust into the situation where I not only had to live them but, also make sure they worked. On the day following Joplin's EF5 tornado, I realized I had to manage every stage of recovery while two or three stages would be active at the same time.

I mentioned in an earlier chapter that I had dealt with storms in my past experience but, nothing of this magnitude. The previous experience helped to a point, but, as stated, there is no manual, no book with specific directions one can follow in such a wide scale destructive event. I had to feel my way through these four stages. Luckily, I had a core group of five to ten upper-level management people around me at all times to aid in the management of the disaster. While I had a hand in all four stages, I drew on the team's management strengths and experience directly, at the appropriate times, to help Joplin through the process in dealing with the disaster and recovery process.

Step One: Search and Rescue

The first step in the disaster recovery process is search and rescue. For us, this was the frantic two week time period following the crisis. As you might expect, the safety services and Lane Roberts, the police chief and Mitch Randles, fire chief, were essential to me and the city as a whole during this phase. Instinctively, we knew our first reaction was to help people in a setting that has to be as close to a war zone as you can get. Fortunately in this effort, we had the help of the citizens themselves and thousands of first responders. Clearing debris from the streets, accomplished by public works crews, was essential in this effort. It was the initiative that made all others possible.

I am convinced there are thousands of heroic stories and efforts that occurred during the stage of search and rescue, most of which, I'll never even hear about. One story that deserves recognition tells of the selfless acts of Christopher Lucas. President Obama shared Christopher's story with the audience during his address at Missouri State University on May 29th.

Christopher Lucas, a young man in his late 20's, was working as a manager at the Pizza Hut restaurant on Rangeline Road when the tornado alarms sounded. Upon hearing the sirens, he gathered his customers into the walk-in refrigerator and saw that he couldn't fit inside. So, he strapped himself to a bungee cord while protecting the customers by holding the door closed. Unable to protect himself from the fierce winds, Christopher sacrificed his own life, to save others. His spilt-second decision was heroic, and, in my mind, the foremost example of "The Miracle of the Human Spirit."

Step Two: Debris Removal

The second stage of Joplin's disaster recovery process was debris removal. Many disaster response experts would probably argue that Search and Recovery should be the second step, but based on the advice I received from FEMA Director Craig Fugate, we never really used this step. In a real sense, we combined Search and Recovery with Search and Rescue and used spotters until there was no possible hope of finding survivors—never wanting to give up hope. Who was I to say that some miracle wouldn't happen? I prayed for one to occur.

Looking back, it was Tuesday afternoon, May 24th, when the last remaining human survivor was pulled from the wreckage; within a 72 hour time span following the tornado. Mitch and I were surprised and pleased that we didn't have a single sighting of human remains in all 300 million cubic yards of debris removed. There were, however, some animals pulled out alive at the two week point. I'm sure those animals were glad to see daylight when they were rescued. I was told later how they lapped up water as quickly as the rescuers could bring it to them.

I have spoken extensively about the debris removal process which took 68 days and was quite a challenge to manage. Whereas, the initial phase was energized by pure adrenaline, the debris removal tested stamina and mental toughness as the days wore on. Jack Schaller of the Public Works Department and Leslie Jones from the Finance Department managed the daily efforts in this stage of working with FEMA, the National Guard, and mostly the Corps of Engineers. Both did an amazing job with Leslie working the details and procedures while Jack concentrated on in-field operations. The three of us would meet as needed, but at least two to three times a week we met to discuss many things, including our overall process as reflected on the maps and to evaluate and critique our efforts. We also toured the Expedited Debris Removal (EDR) areas to measure our progress.

I recognized some interesting dynamics going on in Joplin which other communities may want to be aware of. I had been told of psychological studies detailing the emotional stages a community goes through after a disaster of such epic proportions. I requested copies of the studies, but, never received them, which was interesting in light of all the other information that poured in.

This leads to the Tenet #8 of disaster response: Be aware of the psychological mood of the community. Consider using and referring to fixed dates for goals that are prominent and realizable; goals the community can rally behind. At some point the community goes from a sprint to a marathon mode and for us it occurred after meeting the August 7th EDR deadline and assuring that schools would reopen for students by the August 17th deadline.

After the acquired 600 manufactured housing units were fully occupied, there was another natural letdown. I didn't have any significant new goals established, although there were a lot of smaller ones. We had cleaned an amazing amount of debris up and the kids were back in school. People saw a vast wasteland of approximately six square miles with virtually no structures on it and were logically asking what next?

There were other dynamics at play. People from outside Joplin assumed that since the debris was cleaned up everything must be back to normal at City Hall. This, combined with another development I call the Count Ciano factor, were challenges. I love quotes and couldn't help but recall Ciano's quote: "Victory finds 100 fathers, but defeat is on orphan."

We were getting high marks for how we were handling things, not only by FEMA, but were being used as an example in the national press of an example of where things worked well in a world where there was a lot of dysfunction. People were coming forward wanting to be recognized for specific efforts or programs. I struggled with how to refocus our community, to make them realize the hard work of rebuilding was yet to begin; we couldn't afford to lose our sense of urgency. To be honest, I was a little shocked that people didn't understand this, but the stark reality was that they didn't.

Step Three: Demolition

The third step in the disaster recovery process is demolition. This is confusing to many because logically most people would consider this part of debris removal. Unfortunately, FEMA does not, unless it is perceived as an imminent threat. Approximately 1500 of the 7500 storm-impacted structures in Joplin had some form of permanent structure on them. About 1000 or so of these had two or three walls, but were far too gone in terms of overall damage to rebuild them. These structures sat on foundations. Some had basements, as well as steps, driveways, pools and other related structures that needed to be removed as well.

Although FEMA can't pay for these demolition efforts, they do have volunteer groups they work with that have equipment to do this for the impacted community. The city then awards a contract to have the remnants of the structure removed from the curb to the landfill. Those that intend to rebuild at the same place are asked to let the city know of their plans and are exempt from the entire process. The whole thought behind the effort, is to clean up all the properties in a timely manner, and not to inhibit redevelopment by having these visual reminders of the tornado remain on the landscape.

Step Four: Rebuilding

The last stage of disaster recovery efforts is the rebuilding effort. This will be the longest of the four stages and the one we can least control. We can't force someone to rebuild their house, but the city can create incentives and produce an environment where people want to do just that. I think we have accomplished much in the rebuilding process in Joplin, by keeping people nearby. Many started rebuilding without the final report being advanced by the CART committee. Unfortunately, disaster recovery isn't a perfectly-timed process and at the time of this writing approximately 40% of all properties have secured permits to repair or rebuild their properties.

A lot of properties have been tied up by developers interested in the low-income housing tax credits (LIHTC) made available by the state to the Joplin area. While the intentions of the state were good ones, I can't help but wonder where those people are that sold or optioned their properties to developers for those competitive LIHTC funds. Our involvement in the extent of this process will be governed by the overall housing study we commissioned early on. I would highly recommend any city to pursue a housing study early on after a disaster because it provides bearings and goals for the different types of housing needed.

The City of Joplin is mindful of the uncertainty that still exists in the minds of our citizens. We know from talking to bankers that reserves are up, as people sit on their insurance settlements to see what happens in the city as a whole. We are aware of this and work behind the scenes to make things happen to make sure progress continues. We also make sure we message certainties often to allay people's concerns about the future.

We partnered with the local Habitat for Humanity and the affiliate in Tulsa to secure properties for them to construct homes. We presented this in such a manner to serve as a challenge to other nearby affiliates to meet or exceed the Tulsa affiliates efforts.

Television's "Extreme Makeover" Considering Joplin

"Extreme Makeover: Home Edition," the show that creates and builds home for deserving families in record time, were considering Joplin as a possible location for an upcoming show. They eventually would construct seven beautiful homes in the storm damaged area to mark their 200th television episode. I'll fill in the details when we get to the October calendar of events.

We have worked with the state and other entities to develop a tool grid that details all of the incentives and other financial devices that can help citizens rebuild their homes. These tools include low income tax credits, New Market Tax Credits, Community Development Block Grants funding and other programs of assistance.

The City has also developed the first phase of a tree replanting program based on the generous donations of many in the region to help us rebuild our urban forest. Trees in the hard hit areas were uprooted, splintered or completely gone.

With all the rebuilding going on, there is still so much left to complete. There are signs of progress, but what the tornado destroyed in a few seconds will take time to restore. Every time I visit the storm area, I see images of people working, construction crews swinging hammers, new lumber in piles, bricks being laid; evidence of a community determined to not let the tornado win.

Joplin's Comeback Takes Shape

"Like everybody else in America, the coverage of the devastation in Joplin was just heart-rending. We wanted to figure out a way to create some funds that were immediate..."

—Sheryl Crow, Recording Artist/Songwriter, from Kennett, Missouri. Donated her 1959 Mercedes convertible for action to benefit devastated Joplin schools.

While the city as a whole was making significant progress with debris removal, we were all concerned about the switching of Army Corps contractors and the impact this could have on achieving our goal. The switch was not our choice, but a decision that FEMA and the Army Corps made on a federal level. However, I kept daily tabs on the numbers of lots being cleared to insure we were progressing at an acceptable pace. I had to play the role of the bad cop at both our weekly Monday morning meeting and in personal conversations with Jack Schaller from the Public Works Department. Jack in turn passed on our dissatisfaction to the Corps of Engineers in regard to the numbers dropping after the transition.

Tuesday morning, July 5th, saw us holding, in conjunction with FEMA, a kickoff event for the group manufactured housing unit (MHU) site across from the Joplin Regional Airport. It was unbelievably hot that day, as we announced the start of an around-the-clock effort at Hope Haven Park and Jeff Taylor Memorial Park to ready 346 pads for staging of the manufacturing housing units. The second park was named for the fallen Riverside, Missouri police officer, who would be honored at a memorial service that next day at the Safety Center building. This was the officer mentioned earlier who was struck by lightening while directing traffic at 20th and Connecticut on the 23rd of May. I felt great empathy for his family in attendance at the service, especially his young son who sat through the entire service, not fully realizing how his life had been impacted. As I was fighting back the tears, I offered up a silent prayer for the young boy.

Later that day, we had a four hour long council meeting to review each of the 457 properties in question that still needed to have debris removed. The public process can be tedious and this procedure was required under Missouri statute to allow an opportunity for those who hadn't made provisions to get their property cleared; giving the owners one last attempt to stop the demolition process. It made for a long day.

ABC's "Extreme Makeover: Home Edition" Coming to Joplin

The remainder of that first week in July was full of meetings that had become customary. One of the more interesting meetings was the one with the Senior Locations Manager for ABC's "Extreme Makeover" show mentioned earlier. He met me in a room full of city staff that would assist in efforts should the town be chosen as a location. Realizing what this could mean for Joplin, I assured John the City of Joplin would do whatever it took to make his show successful if they came to Joplin. He had been careful to point out, despite my reassurance, that the decision had not yet been made.

I had a couple of meetings on Friday, July 8th, setting the stage for a couple of long-term financial tools that could provide great assistance to Joplin. The first was the Community Development Block Grant (CDBG) which would provide funds from the Federal Government and the second was an application for a unique tool called New Market Tax Credits. I also made the decision to open up the western section of the city for new construction for residential purposes. We had been monitoring the progress of the clean-up on the daily maps and based on the progress, we were able to open this section up after only eighteen of the sixty days had expired. We had made a pledge to the citizens that we would lift the moratorium as soon as possible and I felt that we were honoring our word.

The following week I moved from debris removal mode to that focus on rebuilding. I started to spend more time with Sam Anselm, the Assistant City Manager, and Troy Bolander, Planning Director developing the grid for listing tools and resources to help citizens rebuild their homes. Additionally on Tuesday July 13th, we had the first meeting between the CART group and the citizens of Joplin to gather input as to what they wanted to see in the redevelopment plan. We also made a second attempt, via phone, to get Habitat International involved in our rebuilding efforts, which met with about the same result as we got our first time. I'm still waiting.

Infection Scare

About this time, we began to receive information about several people injured in the storm having a rare fungal infection called Cutaneous Mucormycosis. As of early July there had been twelve confirmed cases of this infection according to the Center for Disease Control (CDC), of which five had deadly consequences. A CDC investigation team traveled to Joplin to look into the infection, and then returned to Atlanta with a lot of unanswered questions. Evidently, their findings were consistent with other similar type circumstances given the wind velocity present in Joplin that day.

Scorching Temperatures for July

I was still working everyday of the week, but by mid July, I was trying to be home more on Saturdays and Sundays. My average work week had dwindled to about 75 hours. Leslie, Jack, and Troy were with me virtually every step of the way. We were all exhausted, but we didn't have a choice but to continue to push ourselves; there was still so much left undone.

The third week in July was a relatively normal week as we continued with the debris removal effort and laid the ground work for our rebuilding efforts. The volunteers continued to come and work despite the scorching heat. The average high temperature in June was over 91 degrees, when the historical average was 85 degrees. July was hotter with several days of 100 plus degrees.

Requests Coming In For Speakers

Joplin's leaders, including our office, began to receive many requests or invitations to speak throughout the country. That was a problem, because we still had an incredible amount of work to do and the people actually managing the crisis were those most qualified and capable of speaking. This illustrates Tenet #9 of disaster management: Use the attention created by the event to benefit the community. Don't be overwhelmed or victimized by it. We knew we had a bully pulpit, but we needed to use the opportunities wisely and not let the attention use *us*.

Because of the national and even worldwide attention focused on Joplin, I was able to get an audience and request help from people who normally wouldn't be available to us. The other side of the coin, however, is the need be prepared for the onslaught of people that want *your* time. You had to perform a prioritization exercise by saying no, or delegating others to meet certain requests for speakers; putting off invitations for the time being and accepting others. If you don't manage this demand for your time, it will end up enveloping you and detracting you from, or even interrupting community recovery efforts.

As far as managing the speaking requests, all requests coming in for Mayor Woolston, Lynn Onstot, the Public Information Officer, and me, were scheduled through an organized Speaker's Bureau. We established a core group of my small staff who had the time and ability to handle the presentations. We then established general guidelines to govern the presentations and began review of the requests with this structure in place.

Plans to Mark the Six Month
Anniversary of Tornado

On Friday, July 22nd, I was involved with the first meeting of the Memorial Committee, made up of a core group of people throughout the community. This group, later decided, after consulting with a mental health professional, to hold the event on November 22nd, the six month anniversary of the tornado.

I also made the decision that 30th day into the residential construction moratorium, to lift the rebuilding ban from the area near St. John's Hospital to Main Street. After monitoring the maps on a daily basis, I felt we had made enough progress in this area to open it up for new construction. Effectively, two thirds of the Expedited Debris Removal (EDR) area was now open for residential construction.

On Sunday July 24th, the first manufactured housing units at the group site by the Joplin Regional Airport were occupied. This was sixty-two days after the tornado and enabled housing assistance to those in need and provided us a better opportunity to retain our citizenry. We were very proud of our efforts to get these units in as quickly as we did, through a determined team effort.

That last week in July saw us involved with ongoing efforts on many fronts. We continued to meet with CART leadership to discuss the evolution of their report. Their effort had gained traction with the installation of Jane Cage, a local businesswoman as their Chair. She proved to be a bright and capable leader. Our position in the city administration was that he would help anyway we could in the development of the plan but we were careful to not control its overall development. I believed in the integrity of the citizen-driven process and did not want to taint the eventual product.

Finishing Out July

I had been asked to write a Foreword for a book about the tornado published by the Kansas City Star titled, "Joplin 5:41," which I viewed as an honor. I focused mainly on the contributions of the registered volunteers, which now stood at 75,000. The document was not a long one but, one in which I put a lot of thought. I hoped I contributed in some small way to the success of that book. I received two copies of Joplin 5:41" in October. I had seen the book for sale at a book store in Springfield, the week before, but did not realize it was the Kansas City Star book. I thought the book was well done and documented in a professional way the horrors of 5-22-11.

The remainder of that last week in July was spent on an unsuccessful effort to get FEMA to pay for the economic development aspect of the demolition effort. We also began compiling our CDBG request to send to Senator Roy Blunt's office. That effort consisted of meeting with staff to brainstorm Joplin's "unmet needs." Finally, during that period, I started holding council briefings again, which were meetings set prior to a scheduled council meeting with groups of two of our elected officials to review the agenda and discuss other developments in the city. I had suspended those meetings in the aftermath of the storm, but decided it was time to reinstate them. It would give me an opportunity to update and discuss recovery efforts with the city council who are my direct bosses.

A long, hot July came to an end, but we were still working many hours, often well into the night, to insure Joplin's comeback.

Deadlines Met: A Total Team Effort

> "Individual commitment to a group effort–that is what makes a team work, a company work, a society work, a civilization work."
>
> —Vince Lombardi, Legendary Football Coach

The busy week of August 1ˢᵗ, 2011 was indicative of the degree of national attention Joplin was receiving due to the tornado. During the course of this week we had two networks in town filming documentaries. We also received a call from a producer for ESPN's "Outside the Lines" segment, requesting an interview. Kathleen Seibelus, the Secretary of Health and Human Services, visited the area during the week, as well. Calls came in from former U.S. Senator Kit Bond and FEMA Deputy Administrator, Rich Serino, and a reporter from USA Today. While opportunities like these helped to spotlight Joplin and our continued needs, we had to keep our focus on debris removal as this was the week designated by President Obama as the deadline to complete that process. We couldn't forget one of the tenets of disaster management in that we had the bully pulpit; however, our most important priority was helping our citizens.

I was monitoring the daily numbers for lots cleared to insure that we would reach our goal. Jack Schaller and I were meeting with Army Corps representatives and with their contractors urging renewed intensity; imploring them to hasten the pace.

I was averaging anywhere from eight to ten meetings a day on a variety of topics. Chris Cotten, the Parks and Recreation Director, was starting to discuss the rebuilding of Cunningham Park with me and others. Chris continued to do a fine job even though, as previously mentioned, he was new to the city. I have to tell this one on Chris. Being new to the job, Chris was not aware of the protocol which called for department heads to immediately report to the EOC in the event of disaster. As a result, on May 22nd he was driving around checking on the parks he was responsible for moments after the storm. He ended up helping St. John's Hospital establish a temporary presence at Memorial Hall, a venue for which he was responsible. My assistant, Sam, called Chris numerous times at his home, leaving recorded messages. We didn't see Chris until the next day. Because he couldn't be reached and didn't make our meeting, more than one person on that following Monday, asked him if he had slept through the tornado.

Living Memorials to the Victims of the Tornado of May 22nd

Over the weekend, I worked on a plan by which the city could honor the citizens we lost by planting a tree in the name of each in Cunningham Park. In that way, their memories would continue to live on for generations to come. The trees were to be planted in what was likely to become our most important park in the city, Cunningham Park. I shared the idea with Chris Cotten at our August 2nd meeting.

August 2nd was a very important day for Chris and the future of the parks system. On that day, citizens in Joplin were going to the polls to vote on whether to support the renewal of a sales tax issue involving both the parks and the storm drainage system. This funding was originally initiated by voter approval in 2001. It was essential in moving Joplin ahead by providing funding for much-needed drainage, in addition to allowing the construction of our new athletic complex as well as other parks' amenities. Shortly after the tornado, the City Clerk had asked me if I still wanted the parks and storm water issue placed on the ballot in light of the storm. My instincts told me to stick to our plans for an August 2nd vote. For good measure, I asked Mayor Woolston for his opinion and he agreed with me. I was glad we didn't change the plan, as Joplin residents approved the renewal of the sales tax by a large margin.

August 7th Deadline Approaching Fast

I was working to finish the Foreword I was asked to write for the Kansas City Star. They had asked me to include thoughts on the volunteer effort in Joplin. It was not difficult to find inspiration, given the incredible numbers of participants. I had to complete this task on August 3rd. That same day, Troy Bolander and I met with the wonderful people from the Tulsa Habitat for Humanity affiliate. They wanted to help Joplin by rebuilding ten homes by the end of 2011 in a very aggressive plan. I was very pleased with the offer made by the contingent from Tulsa's Habitat office.

At the end of the meeting, they looked at me and asked me what concerns I had. Their PowerPoint presentation had detailed, in a very professional document, the need to hit milestone dates in order for the program to work. The only concern I had was the ability to acquire contiguous properties for them to build on by August 15th, which was only 12 days away! Troy echoed the same concern. They had asked us to facilitate the purchase of the land and I knew that acquiring property in the same area, by a developer or any entity, had become the biggest challenge in our rebuilding efforts.

There were a number of reasons for this, including the fact that the owners were dispersed and hard to locate, Low Income Housing Tax Credits (LIHTC) plans tied up many lots, and a speculative fever had overtaken Joplin causing a rush to buy and sell property. In response to our concerns, the Tulsa Habitat people told us the deadline could be pushed to the end of August, but anything past that would delay the project until 2012. We would have to apply Joplin's "can do" attitude to several areas of their proposal in order to make this happen.

The remainder of that first week in August was a series of meetings on a variety of different topics as we continued to monitor our progress to meet our August 7th deadline. We had been turned down in our request for an extension by FEMA, so we had to develop a measured press release, in response to the decision, which explained what implications this would have for Joplin. I was not always the picture of patience throughout this process. We were about seventy-five days into our disaster response and I had taken only two days off from the office during that entire time. I was very tired, but I think I showed some restraint in this instance for which

FEMA was appreciative. I explained to the public, that while we were disappointed the extension was not granted, we still thought we would make the August 7th deadline; and if we didn't for some reason, it wasn't a huge problem.

On Saturday, August 6th, we had our first twenty families moving into the manufactured housing units located at the site across from the airport. There had been a last minute glitch on Friday with respect to the handicapped access to the storm shelters, required to accompany the units. I had to raise a little fuss with FEMA about the delay, in order to get their creativity flowing. They originally had a step necessary for wheelchairs to enter the storm shelter units and they added another lift of asphalt to allow a ramped-entryway effect. The problem was solved and families moved in that weekend.

Deadline Met!

On Sunday evening August 7th, I received a text from Assistant Public Works Director, Jack Schaller, saying the contractor had completed his work and all the lots had been cleared. There was still some debris at the curb, but it was caused by residents clearing what remained of their homes and taking the remnants to the curb. Although we had messaged residents not to do this, it was impossible to police. I was very happy that we had met President Obama's deadline. Removing three million cubic yards of debris in sixty-eight days was a remarkable logistical feat. It was a tremendous group effort. Return visitors to Joplin could not believe the transformation in the appearance of the town.

The week of August 8th began with our CEO meeting at 7:30 a.m. Monday morning. Colonel Patton of the Army

Corps of Engineers confirmed that we had indeed met our objective of completing the EDR on August 7th. I complimented him, Mike Karl from FEMA, and Colonel Ward of the Missouri National Guard on their efforts that enabled the city to achieve this great feat. I returned to the EOC to begin the work week. I was the lone wolf for a few days as Leslie, the Finance Director, had left for a week's vacation and Jack Schaller was tied up in a deposition for two days.

The remainder of the day of the 8th was filled with meetings as usual. I met with representatives from U.S. Senator Roy Blunt's office to clarify a request Joplin was making for CDBG funds to help us with our unmet needs. We held a press conference at 3:30 p.m. to discuss meeting our EDR goals. I think it was my worst performance at a press conference, but, I was exhausted from the hours and pressure felt over the last few days.

The following day I was interviewed by ESPN producer, Scott Harves, for a story to air on the network's "Outside the Lines" show. The story was to focus on the effects of the tornado related to the upcoming season for the Joplin High School football team, since the high school had been demolished. They interviewed both Mayor Woolston and me for background information. I recall being overcome with emotion at one point during the taping and had to turn away from the camera. The show was scheduled to air sometime in October.

Limit Access to the Emergency Operations Center (EOC)

On Wednesday, August 10th, it was the same daily routine with meetings all day long. Troy and I were starting to talk with developers, who wanted letters of support from the city for applications they wanted to submit to the state of Missouri for the tax credits to build affordable housing. With Governor Nixon directing those resources to Joplin this year, we were getting lots of attention. Later in the day, we participated with some state and regional officials out at the Missouri Southern University campus to review the entire operation at the EOC, to see how we could improve efforts in the future. Although I didn't speak that day to the entire group, when we were divided into sub groups for discussion, I did drive home a weakness related to the need to restrict access to the EOC.

This is the Tenet #10 of disaster response: Limit the number of people given access to the actual operations center. Although I think the overall function of the EOC for Joplin went incredibly well, I would highly recommend this to other cities in a similar situation. Be very exacting in who gains entry into the operations center. Not doing so creates unnecessary havoc. Because anyone and everyone could drop by at any time, it was difficult to receive sensitive updates from my department heads. The noise and hubbub at the center, made concentration and focus difficult during times we were making difficult decisions, and in fact, made us vulnerable to those with personal agendas who had no business being in that setting.

"Joplin Globe" Touts Efforts in Joplin

The city was pleased to see a very complimentary article in the local Joplin Globe newspaper on Thursday, August 11th, with quotes from Libby Turner, FEMA's top official in charge of the federal response to Missouri disasters. "It's been an incredible response. The effort here (in Joplin) has been the best organized effort I've ever seen," Libby was quoted as saying. This proved to be a great morale boost for those of us in the EOC. I personally thanked Libby for her kind comments the next time I spoke with her.

Schools Open on Time

The week of August 15th saw the attention in the city shift to the Joplin R-8 school system. They had established a goal of opening the schools on the regular scheduled date of August 17th. One of the primary reasons for doing so was to instill in people's lives a sense of normalcy by enabling the school routine to resume. In order to do this, they had to retrofit a number of existing buildings in the community for use as modern classrooms. The foremost example of this was the former Shopko building at the local mall, which had been vacant since before I had moved to Joplin. This building was to be used for the 11th and 12th graders. Joplin received a great deal of national attention as the R-8 school system achieved their goal to re-open school on their target date. Concurrently, plans were underway for the reconstruction of replacement buildings and repairs to additional schools for an amount in excess of 100 million dollars.

CART Meetings—Citizens Shaping the Future

Tuesday August 16th, was the date of the second public input meeting for the CART process. Various ideas from the prior meeting had been compiled by the CART Committee and presented on display boards to allow citizens to visualize what they would like to see happen. Everyone in attendance was provided adhesive dots to affix to the efforts they thought were most important. This meeting was well attended but, probably wasn't as significant in numbers as the first public meeting.

After reading the narrative summary of the August 16th meeting, I would say the general overriding concern was that citizens wanted to see the city rebuilt in a way that enhances overall appearance of the city. We had a unique opportunity to do that based on the fact that 1/3 of the city was gone. I attribute this desire for aesthetic success to a lot of things going on in Joplin, but most prominently I credit the efforts of our downtown redevelopment project. Citizens were realizing that things didn't always have to look the way they have for years. Our city logo states we are "Proud of our Past... Shaping our Future." It was a very powerful concept for any city to realize a more positive image. Most cities get caught up in what I call the "grass and trash" routine, in that they become immersed in those core functions and fail to actually lead their town to a better tomorrow. Realizing you can make your city into what you want it to be is invigorating and empowering.

The evening of Tuesday, August 16th was dedicated to the announcement of the new location for St. John's Hospital scheduled to take place at our local Holiday Inn. Having been involved on the selection committee, I knew what location had been selected. From the talk on the street, I wasn't the only one that knew. This was a hard secret to keep for some. That night they announced they were going to approve the 50th Street and Main site in the southern most part of the city. You may recall how I had favored this location as the best site for the hospital. I had some personal concerns; it was only two stone's throws away from where I lived, but all things considered, it was a good choice.

Something, Sometime Was Bound to Go Wrong

Around this time there was quite a bit of discussion about planning a benefit concert to be held in the Joplin area the weekend of September 11th, marking the ten year anniversary of the terrorist attack on the World Trade Center. The event was tentatively scheduled to be held at the Downstream Casino just outside of Joplin. Our Convention and Visitor's Bureau Director, Pat Tuttle, first brought it to my attention. A nearby promoter from Springfield had been working with a philanthropist in Los Angeles to organize the event. The entertainer names mentioned to me were very well-known artists. I was encouraged about the fundraising opportunity and the chance to get Joplin's name in the news to draw attention to other funding requests, too. To top it all off, we were able to have the famous 9-11 flag in town that weekend. The flag was traveling across the country at important events. I thought we could use the flag's presence to cap off a very unique concert event to benefit victims of the storm.

I was never sure just *how* the concert unraveled, but unravel it did. I had some people telling me that the breakdown was attributed to the promoter in Springfield, who had perhaps portrayed himself to be better connected then he was. Soon the casino pulled out and shortly thereafter, the original concert effort as a whole was cancelled.

Later in early September, we made one last effort to put a patriotic concert together for September 11th at Landreth

Park, a huge open park area to the north of the EDR area. Once again, a group of local citizens were working with the city to plan the event with three goals in mind: to be a morale booster for the city, keep the Joplin name in the public eye to enable us to receive the CDBG funding that we would get in the future, and, hopefully raise money to help storm victims. Through the last ditch efforts of a local businesswoman we were able to schedule country music artist, Travis Tritt, to perform at the park and provide an opportunity to display the 9-11 flag. The lady in charge was to raise sponsorship dollars to pay for the concert; money provided by funds donated by the Community Foundation of the Ozarks which would allow the entertainment to be scheduled. Several members of the committee working on the concert, with me in the lead, had asked the Foundation's Board (tornado fund board for long-term recovery) for the money up front to line up the entertainment with the understanding that all of the pledges would go back into the fund as repayment with additional proceeds in tow. This request was made on September 6th and approved by the group.

Later that night, at an informal council meeting, I explained the funding, asking the city council to enable the city to be the entity through which the money would flow from the Foundation. The Foundation had asked that the city be used as a conduit for the funding. Council's approval was not reported in the local paper, until that Friday and when the story appeared, it set off a wave of negative responses. The concern was a misconception—some thought the money to front the concert would be taken from the storm victims, when in fact that money was to be repaid by the sponsorship pledges.

In the meantime, we had a concert committee meeting early Friday afternoon, preceding the Sunday concert. The lady in charge of planning for the event was prepared to announce she had raised the sponsorship money to pay back the Community Foundation. Any additional money raised would have put that fund in the black and enabled more storm victims to be helped. Unfortunately, Travis Tritt and his management team, hearing of the complaints, pulled out of the event cancelling any further opportunities for more money to be raised. When the Committee read the Tritt web page comments, they became infuriated with the inaccuracies in the account. I urged restraint, "I know it might feel good to lash out and publicize the actual facts, but it would only prolong misunderstanding, and make things worse."

Looking back on how this all happened, I was able to put it in perspective. The community was tired and frustrated and something like this was waiting to happen. I was at fault for not fully considering the emotional side of the loaned money. I only saw the issues related to accomplishing the three stated objectives. In retrospect, we had just achieved two big deadlines: the August 7th EDR goal and the August 17th date for reopening of the schools. We had reached the *marathon* portion of disaster recovery. I hoped this was the low point in the disaster recovery process that experts warned would happen. I took my lumps and pressed on.

On Thursday, August 18th, I had to go the dentist to have a temporary crown replaced. I had tried to make several appointments prior to May 22nd, but, had to cancel several times due to my busy schedule. Because the crown had been in place for such a long time, the dentist found it difficult to remove. He had to do everything short of sticking his shoe in my mouth for leverage, but it finally came loose. As I left his office, I was looking forward to the next day, Friday the 19th. It would be my first work day off since the storm and only my third day off from working the recovery since May 22nd. Part of me felt guilty about taking the day off, but I realized my weariness was doing more harm than good, and my family was taking the brunt of it. I had to try to get some rest and restore a little normalcy to my life.

Three Month Anniversary

Monday, August 22nd marked the three month anniversary of the Joplin tornado, the deadliest tornado in the United States since 1947. The last week of August started out on a pleasant note. Walgreens had two ribbon cuttings, celebrating the re-opening of two of their stores destroyed by the tornado. I was unable to find a parking place within two blocks of either store; a good indication that both events were well attended. These ribbon cuttings were important for Walgreen's patrons, but also served as salve for the psyche of Joplin residents. Businesses re-opening and the many rebuilding efforts were symbols of commercial recovery in a town wholly dependent on commerce.

Earlier in the day, we had met with representatives from "Extreme Makeover: Home Edition" who were still exploring the possibility of filming one of their shows in Joplin. I realized the potential benefit to Joplin of this kind of exposure and told them once again that the city would do whatever was necessary to make their efforts a success if they selected Joplin.

On Thursday August 23rd, our local state Senator, Ron Richard, former Mayor of Joplin, asked me to testify via telephone to a Disaster Recovery Senate Committee meeting being held at the state capitol in Jefferson City, Missouri. Basically, I just provided an update of our recovery efforts and responded to any questions. I wasn't sure what to expect, but I knew Ron was a vocal advocate for Joplin, so I knew I would be treated fairly by the committee.

Later that same day, I met with representatives from St. John's Hospital to review some conceptual ideas they had developed early on for the re-use of their existing property. They had indicated early on a desire to give their property to the city, but we had not discussed any details since that point in time. Their plan called for setting aside property for the Joplin school system. I had heard rumors to that effect, so I was not surprised to see that reflected in the plan which included a stipulation that a memorial garden area be created. This garden would honor the memory of the destroyed hospital building and surrounding grounds. But nowhere in the hospital's plan did I see where property was set aside for museum purposes; the museum we had discussed which would be dedicated to remembering the May 22nd tornado. Nor were they aware of *our* plans for Cunningham Park directly across the street from the property we were discussing. I had to be tactful in responding to the plan they presented to me. They were talking about giving the city land, so I couldn't be too forceful in my response as I had no leverage with which to do so. I tried to tactfully explain the ideas we were discussing with respect to Cunningham Park and the museum and my thoughts on connecting the two via an overhead walkway. We were planting the 161 trees, installing water features to reflect the regenerative properties of that element, building a volunteer memorial in Cunningham Park. They were very kind and accommodating in their responses and I left with the feeling that they would make adjustments to their plan given the input they had just received.

$1.3 Billion Requested

The following day city staff put the finishing touches on our CDBG requests to Senator Blunt's office. We had compiled our "unmet needs" and infused a little forward thinking to generate a list totally just short of 1.3 billion dollars. Most of these funds were geared to helping the homeowners rebuild, but reflected infrastructure needs, too. This dollar amount reflected the amount other cities with similar disasters had received, per information from officials of the Department of Housing and Urban Development. I have mentioned before this information: The 9-11 recovery efforts received $3 billion, the Katrina disaster received 2 billion dollars, and the 2008 Midwest floods were allocated $800 million. In light of these numbers, $1.3 billion seemed reasonable to me. Unfortunately for Joplin, our request came while ongoing discussions about fiscal restraint on the federal level were taking place.

Later on August 24th, U.S. Senator Clair McCaskill revisited Joplin to get an update on our efforts. I was asked by her lead team to moderate a panel discussion of local leaders providing the senator with the information she was seeking.

It has a little bit of a challenge as I didn't know many of the people at the table, but we muddled through.

Special Memory for Me and Miles

On Friday August 26th, representatives from Joplin were invited to attend the Governor's Cup pre-season game between the Kansas City Chiefs and the St. Louis Rams at Kansas City's Arrowhead Stadium. I was given tickets to hand out to deserving city employees and it was nice to get away from everything we had been dealing with, if only for an evening. As an added benefit, I had been asked to participate in the coin toss before the game. After discussing with my wife, we decided that my twelve year old step-son, Miles, would accompany me onto the field. He was not a sports fan like my four year old son, Ryan, but we reasoned that Miles would remember this once in a lifetime honor, unlike Ryan, who would be too young to recall it.

Miles and I were brought down to the field during a flurry of pre-game activity to prepare for our roles mid-field. There were kids from Joplin's youth football program on the sidelines so we were comfortable in our surroundings. The entire Kansas City Chief's administrative staff was present. At the proper time, we followed the Chiefs mascot to mid-field, to participate in the coin toss. Team captains Eric Berry and Jon McGraw were on the field and both reached to shake our hands. Following the coin toss, we went back to the sidelines where Chiefs head coach; Todd Haley went out of his way to shake our hands. Miles and I made our way off the field to find the rest of the Joplin contingent sitting in the end zone area. Following the half time ceremony which called attention to Joplin's efforts and the AmeriCorps volunteers, Lois and I made our way to the owner's box to meet up with Mayor Woolston. "Well, we may have trouble getting you back to Joplin; you look very comfortable and relaxed in this setting," I joked. On the field, the Chiefs weren't playing very well, so I stayed away from Clark Hunt, the owner of the Chiefs, whom we had met earlier.

"Extreme Makeover" Project Still in the Works

Monday, August 29th was another full day punctuated by a special council meeting that evening. I had interviews with the "Extreme Makeover" crew, who were doing pre-interviews to serve as background for proposal to produce a show from Joplin.

In addition, there were other media wanting interviews that day. I had made myself available for so many it was becoming second nature. Later in the day, we had a meeting with FEMA representatives to discuss how to deal with the multitudes of donations we were receiving, especially clothing. As we had stated, I think part of our success in getting people involved in helping Joplin was to not turn anyone down. What we were starting to discuss now, was the flip side of that aspect was what to do with all the donations left over. We were especially concerned about the mountains of used clothing received. We decided on a general plan to make media pushes to tornado victims to accommodate their immediate needs, followed by a focus on the needs for cold weather attire that would be needed soon. Then we would estimate the amount still on hand and see if we could help out with existing needs in other emergency situations in the country.

That night I got a troubling message from "Extreme Makeover's" Location Manager saying the project is in "Devcon 3," meaning they weren't having much luck assembling the property for the "makeovers." I wasn't entirely sure what Devcon 3 meant, but I knew from his tone that the project was at risk. As mentioned, they had decided to build seven homes instead of their typical one per show, given the level of devastation we had experienced. They had local people with whom they worked, but were experiencing the same problems we were facing with assembling or purchasing the property as sites for the homes. I called him back and assured him we would make it happen.

The next day, I put city staff on the task and they worked with a real-estate agent, the Economic Security group in town and "Extreme Makeover" to acquire the property for the project on Connor Avenue, just a few blocks from and within sight of St. Johns Regional Hospital and Cunningham Park.

Late in the day, August 30th, the United Way committee of which I am a part, convened to approve the property acquisition on Kentucky Avenue to enable the Tulsa Habitat for Humanity group to have the property to assist ten Joplin families. We had been able to accomplish the property acquisition by the end of August. I was thankful for the cooperation and support of my fellow board members and pleased that we had the pieces in place for two major housing initiatives. My job was to instill confidence in residents and businesses alike so they would feel comfortable about investing in Joplin's future. I was confident that the "Extreme Makeover" project and Tulsa Habitat for Humanity would help provide the assurance that Joplin was coming back bigger and stronger.

The Joplin Globe printed an article on August 30th, saying insurance companies had paid out two billion dollars in claims so far as a result of the tornado. I was sure that number would rise.

Representatives from Tornado Ravaged Tuscaloosa Come to Town

The last day in August was highlighted by a visit from representatives from Tuscaloosa, Alabama. Their city had experienced an EF4 tornado in late April and they felt a meeting between the two cities could be helpful. They brought a group of about seven people to Joplin, led by their Mayor, Walter Maddox. We had a great visit, starting with a group discussion at City Hall and highlighted with an inspection of the EDR area. They shared stories which were eerily similar to ours. One unique aspect of the Tuscaloosa situation was that their weather forecasters were able to warn people early that morning of the storm that had a 45% chance of developing into a tornado later that day. As a result, they were in lockdown, which they thought was instrumental in limiting the loss of life. Their fatalities numbered 52. Another big difference is that the Alabama tornado was more extensive in overall area than the one we experienced, which hit primarily Joplin and nearby Duquesne. I had to leave the group's meeting in early afternoon for another meeting but, before I left Mayor Maddox and I agreed to urge our Federal legislative contingent to work together to facilitate funding from Washington to our respective cities.

As August was coming to an end, I thought back over the past three months. In some ways, it flew by, but, in other ways, especially where government red-tape and funding was concerned, time seemed to drag by. I was driven to seek and find the means whereby our city would not only survive, but thrive. Joplin deserved that chance.

No Trees in the EDR

"You could hear everything go. It tore the roof off my house, everybody's house. I came outside and there was nothing left. There were people wandering the streets, all mud covered. I'm talking to them, asking if they knew where their family is. Some of them didn't know, and weren't sure where they were. All the street markers are gone."

—Joplin Globe reporter, Jeff Lehr

The month of September started off with a series of meetings regarding the reconstruction of Cunningham Park, the one hardest hit by the tornado. Like most of our undertakings, we had several groups step forward wanting to help. In this instance, it was a group of regional landscape architects that met with us. I tried to relay to them the three general things we wanted to accomplish at our six months memorial event to provide them some insight to assist them in their design for Cunningham Park. From that input, they were able to develop a proposed overall concept for the park that we refined over time. Cunningham Park was quickly becoming hallowed ground for a number of reasons, including the fact that it was our city's oldest park and was near St. John's

Hospital where the storm was believed to have elevated in strength from an EF4 to an EF5 tornado. Additionally, you may recall, it had been the location for our early press conferences and the site for the observed moment of silence at the one week mark following May 22nd. Because of all those factors, I believed the re-design was extremely important in our rebuilding process.

Late in the day on September 1st, I met with Fire Chief Randles and Emergency Coordinator Keith Stammer to discuss changes to the EOC facility at the Public Safety Building. My biggest concern stemmed from Disaster Response Tenet #10, which emphasized controlling access to the EOC itself. Based on my earlier direction to these employees, they had developed ideas to remedy this problem, mainly through the use of doors in both locations and monitoring access through them. I immediately approved their recommendations.

We also discussed, two long term ideas I had developed as a result of the tragedy experienced by our community:

The first was my commitment to pay our thanks forward in future disasters, by developing a crack team of first responders to be in the "first ones out of the bay" in subsequent disasters in our country. Joplin owed so much to so many, and as long as I was managing the city, I wanted to be sure we could be counted on to payback others by applying the knowledge and experience we had learned from this horrible situation.

The second idea I had stumbled across, was to take advantage of the reputation we had developed for excellence in emergency management by establishing a third component to go along with police and fire training at our developing safety center for emergency response training. I reiterated these two goals to Keith and Mitch, but I knew it would take a while for them to develop these concepts.

The first week in September was full of meetings working on developing incentives to assist Joplin's residents in the reconstruction of their homes and to provide tools for businesses to rebuild. We were working with a law firm out of St. Louis to develop legislation for the state legislature to consider in an upcoming special session. The legislation would provide incentives for businesses to jump start the recovery. We also had been asked to prioritize our "unmet needs" in regard to the community development Block Grant (*CDBG)* requests we had sent to Senator Blunt's office. Realizing the emphasis that the Federal government was now placing on responsible spending, I was not the least bit surprised by this request.

Joplin "Extreme Makeover: Home Edition" Scheduled for January Airing

"Extreme Makeover: Home Edition" was finally coming to Joplin. Their 200th episode was scheduled to be two hours long and was to air in January, 2012. On Wednesday, September 7th, we had another meeting with representatives from the show. As stated previously, they had decided to try something new given the level of destruction in Joplin. They would be in town starting October 14th through the 27th and construct seven homes on Conner Avenue in that short span of time. There were a lot of details to be decided prior to this massive effort.

Later that day on September 7th, we met with a regional developer at the Chamber of Commerce offices, who was expressing a significant interest in rebuilding Joplin. I listened intently to their discussions regarding their credentials, a list of prerequisites for determining choice of individual locations, and I tried to encourage them to consider Joplin due to the 270,000 visitors per day, in addition to the two million annual guests visiting the nearby Downstream Casino. I told them the challenge in any redevelopment plan was to find something for these visitors to do at night to keep them in Joplin and to get people visiting the casino to come into town, too.

Talking Up Joplin's Needs and Football with Bernie Kosar

I had nine meetings scheduled on Thursday, September 8th. The day full of meetings started with one scheduled early that morning with Tami Longaberger of the Longaberger Basket Company out of my native state of Ohio. My administrative assistant was a great fan of Longaberger baskets and a sales representative for the company. Through that connection, Tami became aware of Joplin's plight. Accompanying Tami on her visit to Joplin was her boyfriend and former Cleveland Browns and Dallas Cowboys quarterback, Bernie Kosar. Having managed my first city in northeast Ohio in the late 1980's, I was a long time fan of Bernie Kosar and his football achievements. Bernie and Tami and the group that accompanied them had just toured the storm area when I met with them at City Hall. They were in town to show support and to hold a fundraising benefit for storm victims at the Downstream Casino. We talked at some length about the storm and what they could do to help us. We also spent a little time talking football with Bernie during lunch at a local restaurant.

On the same day, we made the announcement that Tulsa Habitat for Humanity was coming to town to build ten homes. We had secured money for the properties from the United Way tornado fund and had purchased the properties right before the end of August. They would start their project the day after "Extreme Makeover" left town, so I was pleased to have two back to back projects demonstrating progress on the residential front.

Since the Travis Tritt concert was cancelled, the 9/11 flag was being displayed at both Cunningham Park and on the campus of Missouri Southern University. It was an honor to have it in Joplin commemorating the tenth anniversary of 9/11.

During the second week of September Planning Director, Troy Bolander and I met with developers interested in low income housing tax credits (LIHTC). As a reminder, these were tax credits made available by the State of Missouri to developers interested in building affordable housing in Joplin. It was a competitive process and the interested developers were asking the city for letters of support to go along with their applications due to the state. A large majority of the statewide funding for these credits had been directed by Governor Nixon to Joplin to help with our rebuilding efforts. The credits would create incentives for rebuilding our city. I met with a few of these developers myself, while Troy met with many more. Each of the developers had tied up anywhere from 50 to 75 properties by either securing an option to buy the tracts, or in some instances having already bought the parcels. Troy had indicated he expected 15 to 20 applications, which were due on October 15th.

If each developer had tied up a similar number of parcels, it made me wonder where these people that had owned or optioned the land were living and where they would end up? I was actually worried that an effort like this with good intentions would serve to reduce our population base. According to the housing study, we knew we needed 3,100 new structures, with 1,700 being single family residences and 840 market rate rentals and 560 affordable units. Most people assumed those that needed the affordable housing were the people living at the group site at the airport location.

About this time, we were starting to flesh out the details of the demolition phase. We still had about 200 structures, in various stages of destruction, standing on foundations throughout the city. In addition, we had about 1,400 properties that had only the foundations, crawl spaces, and basements left. All of these structures needed to be removed, if the property owners did not intended to rebuild their homes. If the structures were left standing they would not only be a hazard, but serve as a reminder of the tornado and have a debilitating effect on people choosing to rebuild. We started to message a deadline of October 15th for owners to let us know what their plans were for the property or we would step in to address the situation.

One More Added to Death Toll

On Wednesday, September 14th, we received a ruling from the coroner on a death reflected in an obituary in the local paper that had raised the death toll from the tornado. The process we had set up earlier, called for the coroner to make such a determination. Our flow of information on any patients still in the hospital had completely dried up, so when we heard of any new developments related to possible related deaths (usually from the paper) we had the police department meet with the coroner to make a determination. We hoped this would be the last time we had to use this process. Again, we already had the dubious distinction of having the highest death total, by far, from any tornado since the National Weather Service started keeping official records in 1950.

Planning the Six Month Memorial Event

The remainder of the second full week of September was spent in meetings on a number of topics including the Memorial Committee. We had selected November 22nd, for the six month anniversary of the storm, as the date for our memorial service. The committee had decided that our goals that day were threefold:

1. We wanted to pay tribute to the 161 citizens we had lost. This would include memorializing the lives of those lost by planting 161 trees in Cunningham Park. It was also an idea that had practical benefits, as there was not a tree left standing in the park.

2. We wanted to dedicate a memorial to "The Miracle of the Human Spirit" and the 100,000 plus registered volunteers that had come to Joplin to help us.

3. We wanted to look to the future, by unveiling two water features; a pond and a fountain, to highlight the regenerative and growth-related properties of water.

Thanks to Libby Turner

On Wednesday the 14th of September, I had a meeting with Libby Turner, the FEMA officer-in-charge of their efforts in Joplin. She was being transferred back east, closer to her home, and she wanted to have a final meeting. She was very complimentary of the efforts of the City of Joplin and FEMA's overall experience in town. Libby was a gracious, capable lady and I admired her professionally and I told her as much. Even though we didn't get everything we had asked for, Joplin's overall experience with FEMA was a positive one. She gave me a U.S. Department of Homeland Security coin, with the FEMA Coordinating Officer insignia on the flip side to commemorate our efforts.

The CART Process Was On-Going

The week of September 19th was like most others, with a flurry of meetings on a variety of different subjects. We were definitely in the marathon stage of disaster recovery and were holding a number of meetings to enable citizens to develop ideas in the form of projects to be presented at a later date. One of these efforts was the CART (Citizen's Action Recovery Team) report. At this point, a tentative decision had been made to present the report, for the rebuilding of the storm damaged area, in November. In order to achieve that goal, a great deal of work had to be performed in order to assimilate the public input into a workable plan. I am not sure all impacted parties could say so, but, I had been very careful to try to keep this process as pure as possible by not influencing its content. The intent of the effort was for it to be citizen-driven and, although I responded to requests for advice on the process, I think I was able to let the report develop on its own. The last full week in September, the CART committee held a three hour long exercise at a local church to translate the citizens input into projects.

The CART process was important in and of itself, but, would be even more important if we could land some of the CDBG appropriations we were requesting. I had some of the CART ideas advanced by our citizens in mind, when I worked with staff to develop our requests. These funds could provide the resources to bring some of the CART ideas to reality. I was in dialogue with Senator Blunt's office to refine our requests to give him a product he could sell in Washington, given the financial and political realities present in our nation's capital. In my mind, our requests were consistent with what I believe was one of the top two core responsibilities of our federal government; to provide for our national defense and, secondly, and more on point, to help in cases of natural disaster.

We Would Be Known for Our Character

Our local Chamber of Commerce had taken the lead in charting a course for future marketing and economic development efforts. Through a local contact, they had enlisted the help of a New York City advertising firm that had strong national contacts with which we could avail ourselves. We knew that we didn't want to be known as just the "tornado city," but wanted to be defined by the character, strength and determination we had demonstrated in responding to the tragedy. We felt that we could accelerate our recovery process by calling attention to those attributes. The week of September 17th, saw us hold a few meetings and conference calls to develop this new identity that would assist us in our recovery efforts.

"Extreme Makeover" to 'Makeover' Cunningham Park, Too

We were having meetings with the representatives from "Extreme Makeover," trying to define what public projects they would do in October when they were in town to construct the seven homes. I spoke up in this regard, "I think you should concentrate on Cunningham Park since it is such an important site and because it is so close to Connor Avenue where you will be building the new homes."

They liked the idea and concentrated their focus on a new basketball court, playground area and volunteer memorial in the park. These ideas would have to be included in a conceptual plan being developed to present to City Council, at their first meeting in October. We were cutting it pretty close as far as timing was concerned.

Meanwhile, Troy and I were still meeting with developers interested in applying for low income housing tax credits. The level of interest in the program was unprecedented, given our circumstances. We would end up getting 21 applications with an ability to fund four or five projects. A significant number of the applicants wanted to meet with us personally to secure a letter of support.

Exploring New Warning Systems

Although ongoing response to the tornado was our first priority, there was other city business that had to be tended to. On Thursday evening September 20th, we scheduled a budget work-session to review the proposed 2011-2012 Joplin city budget. Usually, we take two nights to review the budget with Council, but this year we got through it in one evening.

We also had individual meetings this week to prepare for the State of Missouri Historic Preservation Conference we would host the first week in November. We had been gaining recognition because of our efforts in our downtown and we were pleased the Conference was coming to Joplin. I was scheduled to speak at the conference and I met with the conference planners to outline my comments.

Fire Chief Randles and I had begun discussions to assess the city's preparations and procedures before and after the May 22nd tornado. We began exploring a storm warning, text-alert idea that had been advanced to me a couple of months following the tornado. I was proud of the fact we had sounded the sirens twice before the tornado; first at 24 minutes prior to the storm striking the city, and then again four minutes before. However, I wanted to explore new ways to provide emergency notification. The National Weather Service had released a report around this time partly based on interviews of Joplin citizens. The report indicated many residents had become desensitized to the warning provided by sirens, which resulted in passive responses. The report reinforced this effect by citing a national statistic; only 24% of the time when sirens sound, is there an actual weather event or threat that takes place. It was human nature for some people to ignore the warnings.

Earlier, we had expressed to FEMA, our desire to use Hazard Mitigation funding for weather radios for our residents. Mitch was also interested in using the loss of two of our five fire stations as a chance to select new locations for them, in order to provide better response time throughout Joplin. Much like we do when sighting early warning sirens,

Mitch had pulled out the circles delineating response times to emergencies from the two new stations.

"Great Day of Service" September 25th

On September 21st, FEMA's Deputy Administrator, Rich Serino, came back to town and made good on a promise to have dinner with me. FEMA had just completed their efforts on a Category 3 Hurricane (Irene) on the east coast, so our meal was interrupted by Rich having to take calls with respect to situations surrounding that event. Intermittently, we talked about the progress we were making in Joplin and I conveyed to Rich that I was pleased with FEMA's efforts.

On Friday, September 23rd we had another meeting of the Memorial Committee to discuss our upcoming November 22nd six month anniversary event. Planning for this Memorial Service was going well. We were ahead of schedule and I expected it to be a very important day in Joplin's history.

The next day, the Kansas City Star book, "Joplin 5:41," a documentary based on the tornado, was due to be released. As mentioned, I had written the Foreword and was honored to be a part of the project.

On Sunday, September 25th, Joplin staged an annual event known as the "Great Day of Service," which is a faith-based event led by a local church that sees volunteers throughout the city giving of their time and efforts to help others. The city is an active partner in this effort, which sees in excess of 2,000 Joplinites cutting grass, trimming trees and weeds, painting buildings, and engaged in a whole host of other tasks. It was fortuitous timing that Time Magazine reporter, Joe Klein, author of the book "Primary Colors," stopped to visit us that day as part of a long road trip he was taking. I was scheduled to meet up with Joe later in the day for a tour of the storm area, but he tracked me down at a picnic-style luncheon being held at Landreth Park. Joe and I, along with his photographer, went to the local Books-A-Million store for coffee so he could get some feedback from me about the previous four months and the recovery process. I enjoyed my discussion with Joe, which concentrated mainly on the spirit of the city and the volunteer-effort. Joe spoke to me at some length, then toured the tornado zone. After his visit, he wrote about his Joplin experiences on his blog, but the actual *Time* magazine article was published in the October 24th, 2011 edition. He recounted conversations he had with me, Jay St. Clair, of the church that organized the "Great Day of Service" and referred to me as "large, quiet and sensitive." I am sure the third adjective surprised some of my employees, and definitely my wife.

My Job … Often a Balancing Act

We had started work on developing a tree program to replace a tremendous amount of urban forest. There is no telling now many thousands of trees we lost in the tornado, but saying the Expedited Debris Removal (EDR) zone was barren would not be an exaggeration. Replacing these trees would be an essential part of the rebuilding effort. Parks and Recreation Director, Chris Cotten and I had finalized our tree program this last week in September. Residents could receive two trees per household, from those that had been donated to us, provided they were from the approved tree list authorized by Council. These were trees that would be consistent with our redevelopment plans and conducive to thriving in our area of the country.

Troy Bolander and I worked to develop a score sheet for the numerous Low Income Housing Tax Credit applications we would be receiving. We had to establish metrics to objectively score the applications. This would build to a head in November, when we would need a special Council meeting to prioritize and rank the 21 applications submitted. We would then send our ranking to the state for final approval.

New programs were constantly being advanced to us by different entities wanting to help in the recovery process. One of these ideas originated from Brad Pitt's "Make it Right Foundation," out of New Orleans. Again, Brad was from nearby Springfield, Missouri and had apparently spent some time in Joplin, visiting relatives as a youth. He and his wife, Angelina Jolie, had already donated financially to our recovery efforts. On Friday, September 29th, Troy and I met with representatives from Brad's foundation who were interested in constructing homes in Joplin utilizing green principles in terms of technology and sustainability. I was impressed by the group's open-mindedness and receptivity and thought it was a good opportunity for Joplin. We were not to the point that we could add them to the "grid," the approved tools and incentives published by residents to use to rebuild their homes, but had established a relationship with the foundation and agreed to develop further ideas.

With respect to the incentive grid, I was worried that the programs were still too complicated for our residents to use successfully. Having worked with these programs in the past, I knew the byzantine rules and regulations could be intimidating at best and knew that not only did people have to know the guidelines, but they had to understand how to apply them to be successful. We met with the local development representative for the state, who generously agreed to have the "grid" printed in the local newspaper. I thought that would help spread the word.

During the last week of September, I reinstituted briefings with council members, which took place two days prior to our scheduled council meetings. It gave me a chance to go over the upcoming agenda with them and cover any other issues with the city that had come up before presenting to the large group. I have yet to meet an elected official who likes surprises and these meetings help me mitigate them. It also affords them a chance to ask me questions. We had discontinued these meetings on an off and on basis because of the tornado, and I had heard there were some complaints about suspending them, so I wanted to address those concerns. My job often seemed like I was managing a delicate and sensitive balancing act; responding to the demands associated with losing a third of your city while attending to and providing service for the other two-thirds at the same time.

Dangerous Lead Levels ... Who Knew?

That week we were thrown another curveball. Joplin's long history as a lead and zinc mining town rose up and bit us in the backside. The area damaged by the storm was not close to the old smelter area of the city, so we never considered there would be a significant threat in terms of lead contaminants. The county and city legislation in effect for this area, urged, but did not mandate, lead testing prior to building. A high lead concentration is known to have an impact on children's mental development at certain levels. Some 19 out of the first 43 properties that voluntarily tested under existing law demonstrated lead levels that exceeded safe limits. The remnants of the mining process evidently had remained present for years after the mining operation ceased in the form of existing chat piles. These piles, which looked like small hills made up of little rocks, were often used for fill-in, prior to basements and foundations being poured. Now, due to construction needs presented by the tornado, these unsafe lead levels had to be addressed.

Even though we thought the information might have a profound effect on our rebuilding efforts, we had to let our citizens know of this development. We did this in the form of a press release and in legislation to Council requiring testing to be performed in the entire EDR area. Council approved this legislation with little discussion. While the lead testing of a property is free in Jasper County, remediating the contaminated soil with new soil was thought to cost anywhere from $3,000-$5,000 per property. In order to assist residents, whose properties tested high, we applied for a grant to the U.S. Environmental Protection Agency for funding. We were optimistic about receiving assistance from them.

The last days of September drew to a close and soon autumn would make its way to the Midwest. I thought how Fall once brought colorful changes to the leaves of the trees once dotting the neighborhoods near and in Cunningham Park. There would be no beautiful orange and golden hues this Fall, but hopefully the area that knew so much devastation would once again have trees glowing with bright leaves for many fall seasons to come.

The Braveheart March

"Joplin has been through so much and everybody has just lost much, but just hearing the compelling stories, everyone has really helped each other and they're ready to rise up and rebuild and that's exactly why we're here."

—Ty Pennington,
Host of ABC's Extreme Makeover: Home Edition

By the first week in October, I was running extremely low on energy and knew I had to get out of the office for a while. I was scheduled to be away for the week of October 10th. So, I spent the first week of the month getting things to the point that I felt comfortable being out for a few days.

Thursday, October 6, and Friday, October 7, I was scheduled to be in Branson, Missouri, for a gathering of the Connect2Culture arts group in Joplin. I was a member of the committee but, due to my duties following the tornado, had been uninvolved since May 22nd. One of the committee members, for whom I have deep respect, had asked me to attend this two-day meeting a month before and I told him I would. I decided to take Lois and our two youngest kids with us so we could stay over for a day and have the closest thing to a vacation we had had in a while.

I had planned to also do some writing the week I was out of the office. I was a little frustrated that I had to turn down an invitation to testify before a Senate subcommittee on the tornado during the week I would be out of the office. Instead I sent Keith Stammer, our Emergency Management Coordinator. I knew Keith would be prepared and represent the city well. Upon his return, he reported back to me in the basement at City Hall and it seemed like he thoroughly enjoyed the experience.

During that first week of the month, I had scheduled a meeting with the Chair of the CART process, Jane Cage. I was able to provide a little advice that I hoped was helpful on the process to present the plan. I was still careful not to influence the projects that were being recommended.

On Wednesday, October 5th, Mayor Woolston and I met with a developer out of Texas who had expressed an interest in playing a large role in the redevelopment of Joplin. I was impressed with the level of research they had done on our city. Their plan was extensive and they indicated they already had about a billion dollars in commitment letters for investments in Joplin. That certainly got our attention.

One of the ideas contained in their plan concerned me. They showed a different location for the Cultural Arts Center than was shown in the Stimulate Progress through Arts, Recreation and Knowledge of the Past (SPARK) proposal. This was an initiative I had proposed a few months before the storm which consisted of converting the Union Depot into the local museum, construction of an arts center, and a town green for a local gathering site. Instead of being located on the northern end of our downtown, the Texas developer had it situated in the storm-damaged area.

Although I realized Joplin had been profoundly impacted by the May 22nd tornado, I wasn't ready to abandon the SPARK concept just yet. After the meeting with the developers, the local contingent stayed afterward to further discuss the plan. I stated that it was impressive but there were a few things reflected in the plan that were inconsistent with initiatives we had already started. Mayor Woolston, realizing the need to move quickly to discuss the thing, asked me to set up a meeting upon my return to discuss these ideas to provide feedback to the developer.

"Wheel of Fortune" Interested in Joplin

Late on the morning of October 5th, Joplin's Convention and Visitors Bureau Director, Pat Tuttle had set up a meeting with a scout team from the "Wheel of Fortune" television show to discuss their interest in filming in Joplin. They weren't sure whether they could find a venue in Joplin large enough to accommodate their needs, but they were headed out to the Missouri Southern University campus to make that determination. I was amazed at the attention we had received as a result of the tornado from news organizations and programs. I made a list of those who had helped bring attention our way:

- Extreme Home Makeover
- Time Magazine

- ESPN's Outside the Lines

- The Nature Channel

- National Geographic

- All Major News Networks

- The New York Times

- British Broadcasting Company

- ESPN's Monday Night Football

- Dan Rather Reports

- The Weather Channel

- National Public Radio

- The Mac Neil Report

- Rush Limbaugh

- Barry Manilow

- Various documentaries

- And, many more ...

Certainly the opportunity to use our "bully pulpit," mentioned in the Ten Tenets of Disaster Response, following the disaster, created the means for many of our needs to be met in short order. You have to be prepared for the rush of attention and then manage it with a clear, concise, and consistent message or it will control you.

Branson, a Nice Getaway … then Back at It

It was nice to get away to Branson and away from the pressures and stress of the ongoing disaster response efforts. We had good discussions at the meetings with Connect2Culture group about Joplin's future as a whole and the role the arts would play in it. I felt as though I was getting lobbied by more than one source to move the Arts Center into the storm-damaged area.

When I returned to work on October 17th, there was a buzz and excitement in the air with the pending arrival of the crews from Extreme Makeover, Home Edition, scheduled to arrive in Joplin that Wednesday. I knew that first day back, I would need to catch up on correspondence received while I was away. My expectations were realized when I discovered piles of mail and 351 Emails awaiting my arrival.

I waded through the Emails as quickly as I could. In late morning, I had an advance camera interview with a crew from Extreme Makeover, who needed some background video for the show. Later that night, we had a customary council meeting with a very lengthy agenda.

The Braveheart March for "Extreme Makeover"

At 3:15 that afternoon, I arrived at Cunningham Park with my assistant, Sam, and Parks Director, Chris Cotten, to prepare to be part of the "Braveheart March." I had seen my first full episode of "Extreme Makeover" on a rerun the night before, so I had an idea of what to expect. Later in the afternoon, we were joined by Mayor Woolston and Fire Chief Randles and his wife. The Braveheart March was the part of the program where all volunteers working on a project would march toward the building site, wearing construction helmets and blue Extreme Makeover t-shirts. The group would be filmed charging toward the work site, encircling both the show's host Ty Pennington and other cast members, along with the families selected to receive the homes. The only problem was the temperature began to drop to below freezing, and was supplemented by a generous wind. This was compounded by the fact that we stood for over four hours before we started the march. We were told they were having trouble rounding up the families.

I hadn't counted the participants, but there had to be at least 750 people in blue shirts. That number started to dwindle as the night went on and the temperature dropped. One of the mutineers did so in a lewd and profane manner, so much so that I suggested to one of our officers to give him a ride downtown. At long last we began to march from the Cunningham pool parking lot area along Maiden Lane toward the remainder of what was left of St. John's Hospital. At that point, we were halted. Most of us that represented the city staff were in the back row. By this time, it was dark and very hard to see even though the Extreme Makeover crews had extra lights operating in the park.

At the direction of the crews, we began our march down the hill to where the families were gathered. We probably had to trot about a football field and a half, to get to the area where the large group encircled the families. I was in the rear and nearly tripped a couple of times going down the hill. I was saved the embarrassment of falling altogether and admit at one point I felt like I was preparing for a skirmish from the Civil War. I had lost contact with the rest of the city group who were part of the large circle. The guys from the city would later kid Mitch's wife, saying she *lost* the city manager as she was the one closest to me in physical proximity. Finally, one of the "Extreme Makeover" staff grabbed my hand and pushed me to the inner circle, as I was one of the people to be interviewed by Ty, the show's host.

That was the first time I had seen the show's host. He looked a little on the nervous side, which maybe had to do with the fact that his task had increased significantly with several families to deal with instead of the usual one, and did I mention, it was freezing?

Mitch Randles, our fire chief, was first to be interviewed by Ty. Mitch had some interesting perspectives to share, as he too had lost his house on May 22nd. In addition, one of his firefighters, Kyle Howard and his family had been selected by the show to receive a house. Kyle had been on duty when the tornado struck and arrived home at his first chance to find his wife and kids huddled in a closet with their home destroyed around them. We were happy for Kyle and his family as a fellow city employee, but we played no role in his family's selection; "Extreme Makeover" handled the selection process.

After Mitch was done, Ty asked who the next person would be and I suggested Mayor Woolston. Mike never talks for very long and when he was finished, Ty motioned for me. I talked about *The Miracle of the Human Spirit* and showed them my wrist band that symbolized that effort. I was doing alright until I looked over at a local builder; usually a pretty calm guy who now was crying, and in response, my voice cracked. Despite that, I made it through the interview then assumed my original position in the circle as Ty talked to others, including my assistant, Sam.

Once that segment was complete, the "Extreme Makeover" crew wanted to film one more charge, so we all went back up the hill to film the Braveheart March once again. Although I didn't check for sure, the temperature had to be in the high 20's and the city staff left after the second march with the exception of Mitch Randles and his wife who stayed a while longer.

Closing Out October with the Big "Reveal"

I mentioned in an earlier chapter that Joplin was chosen as host city for the statewide Missouri Historic Preservation Conference during the first week of November. The Conference was going to be held at City Hall, which is housed in a five-story-high historic building in the center of downtown. I was scheduled to speak at the conference on our downtown redevelopment efforts that we launched over five years ago. Our efforts had been successful in a dynamic transformation of the appearance of our center city and, in turn, enhanced Joplin's overall image. I spent part of the morning of Thursday, October 20, working with a city staff member developing slides for my upcoming presentation to the Conference.

On Friday, October 21, the Memorial Committee planning the six month anniversary of the tornado event met again to finalize the schedule for the November 22nd memorial service. Chris Cotton explained to the Committee his conversation with the governor's aide. After lengthy debate, they decided we had better invite the Governor to speak and Chris and a private sector representative of the committee were assigned to call the aide back to let him know of our decision.

The following day, I had a very busy schedule. We had a giveaway day at Landreth Park for storm victims. For some time, stuffed animals had been sent to us from a young girl in Texas, who had worked to collect them for the Joplin children who lost all of their toys, along with their homes in the Joplin tornado. In addition, there was clothing and household items that were provided for those in need. I got the fun job and worked the stuffed animal table with other city employees.

Following my stint at the park, I went to our local library for a book signing. The Kansas City Star book, "Joplin 5:41", for which I had written the Foreword, was available at the library. The book had turned out well and I was proud to be part of it. I wasn't sure exactly what was expected, but, when I arrived, I was told by the Kansas City Star representatives that they actually wanted me to sign the books beneath my name in the Foreword. The sales were brisk during the time I was there.

My Saturday was rounded out with an appearance at Joplin's first Oktoberfest celebration in downtown. I was asked to make some brief comments kicking the event off and gladly obliged.

On Monday, United States Senator Roy Blunt of Missouri was back in town for an update. Roy had been in Joplin often and had displayed genuine heartfelt concern. I appreciated his personal interest. He was helping us a great deal by advancing our CDBG request for which I expressed our gratitude.

Tuesday the twenty-fifth of October saw me starting to assemble some of my thoughts for the upcoming memorial service, now less than a month away. I had jotted down some notes at various times during the prior months, and began to organize them somewhat. We not only wanted to call attention to the victims of the storm, again thank all volunteers, and point to the future. Later that day, I tried to organize an effort to honor a local World War II veteran by contacting a relative of his I had heard from earlier. We wanted Howard to serve as grand marshal of the upcoming Veteran's Day Parade. He had given so much to his country and to Joplin and we wanted to do something to honor him for all of his efforts.

On Wednesday, October 26, "Extreme Makeover" had completed the seven homes and was ready to reveal them to the families. The recipients had been sent to Disney World for a week and had been isolated from the massive ongoing efforts in Joplin to construct their homes. I had been down a couple of times to witness this amazing feat and even walked through one of the homes, called the 'beach house,' as it was being finished. It was my favorite of the seven. A half pipe skate ramp had even been erected in the backyard of the home to entertain the skate boarding enthusiasts in the family.

While the wait was thankfully shorter than for the Braveheart March, it was still a couple of hours in dropping temperatures before the houses were revealed to the families that day. The wait was broken up by Ty Pennington, the show's host, riding a skateboard the length of the street, high-fiving all of us waiting as he went by. Seven luxurious mobile home units with the selected families inside pulled up once then pulled away just to tease the crowd, I think. They retreated then approached the street where the houses sat again. Finally, the families exited with their view of the homes shielded by the large travel vehicles. The crowd began to chant, "Move that bus, move that bus." Then, the homes were revealed one at a time, from north to south, to the amazement of their new owners. The episode would be "Extreme Makeover's" 200th show and, as noted, was slated to appear early in 2012.

The following evening, "Extreme Makeover" crews would be in Cunningham Park for the final filming for the show surrounding the improvements made in the park. The Extreme Makeover group was working with their sponsors and the many volunteers that had participated in rebuilding the basketball court, the playground area, and the tribute to the volunteers in conjunction with Drury University out of Springfield, Missouri.

The basketball area was to be located close to the intersection of 26th Street and Maiden Lane, almost directly across from the remains of St. John's Regional Hospital. The playing surface was a multi-colored rubberized material, with fencing surrounding the playing surface and spectator seating on the west end. It had a very inviting and vibrant appearance. While waiting for the film crews to arrive, Chris Cotten, my Parks and Recreation Director, and I challenged two guys from the film crew to the inaugural game on the court. We represented the city well by prevailing with five baskets to their one in a "make it and take it" contest.

The show's crews had also installed a full playground set to the north of the basketball court with a façade depicting Joplin's downtown skyline. They installed the playground equipment in a manner that revealed the dates of the tornado from an aerial perspective.

Finally, the volunteer memorial was located in the northeastern area of the park and was reflected in four stone circles radiating out from the center area. The four circles were intended to symbolize the stages of disaster recovery: search and rescue, debris removal, demolition, and rebuilding. In addition, a metal band symbolizing "The Miracle of the Human Spirit" wrist band worn by so many volunteers, was placed on the boundary of the circles. Shards of debris from the tornado were embedded in a display next to the story-board near the base of the exhibit.

Our hope is to raise money for a bronze sculpture to be placed in the center of the first circle as a tribute to the many volunteers who have come to help Joplin. The plan is to bronze actual storm debris items to serve as a touchstone so that the volunteers, survivors, their children, and their children's children can return for years to come and simulate the role many played in the debris removal process. Children would be encouraged to recreate the act of removing the debris and then placing it in the appropriate receptacle. The outer ring depicts the full recovery of Joplin.

Storm Chaser's Video, Startling Images

On Friday, October 28th, I had a meeting scheduled with Jeff Piotrowski, a storm chaser from Tulsa, Oklahoma, who was here in Joplin with his wife, chasing the tornado on May 22nd. Jeff produced a video of the storm that he gave to me when we met. He was accompanied by a local writer and they wanted to talk to me about a project they were working on. He was very animated and extremely excited as he told me his story. After having a chance to watch the video that weekend, I know why.

Jeff explained to me that he and his wife were in Joplin that night. He told me they were traveling on 7th Street and Blackcat

Road right before the storm hit, an encountered Joplin Police Officer Brewer and urged the officer to sound the sirens a second time. He said that he realized the magnitude of what was happening to Joplin because he followed the storm into Joplin.

Jeff was emotional as he described his experience on Iowa Street, over by the high school, following the storm. He said he could hear people trapped beneath the debris calling for help and that he was frustrated in that he couldn't physically get to everyone that needed assistance. Everything Jeff told me bore out in the footage he video taped on May 22nd. It was incredible footage.

Ten More New Homes Underway

At 8:00 a.m. Saturday, October 29th, I went to 23rd and Kentucky Avenue to participate in a wall-raising ceremony for the ten homes the Tulsa Habitat for Humanity was building in Joplin. The turnout was great in that both the dignitaries and many volunteers showed up. I have mentioned previously, the timing worked great because those ten new homes were scheduled to be built in sixteen days with the building to start the day after "Extreme Makeover" had left town.

Weekends had become full of different events related to our recovery efforts. On Sunday, a friend from Ohio, David Martin, was visiting. David and I, along with my step-daughter, Meagan, went to the campus of Missouri Southern to see their men's basketball team, play the Missouri Tigers in a benefit game. Missouri Southern got off to a slow start and ended up losing 114-68.

Joplin: The Miracle of the Human Spirit

"You, the volunteers, are the living embodiment of 'The Miracle of the Human Spirit.'"

—Mark Rohr
From speech marking the 6 month
anniversary of Joplin tornado
November 22, 2011

The most difficult aspect of the horrible aftermath of the May 22nd tornado, was, of course, dealing with the loss of life. The broken, crushed, and muddied bodies of men, women, boys and girls pulled from the debris will linger in the memories of those who found them. I knew this would be something I had to deal with personally from the instant I saw the two deceased passengers in the minivan while running up Main Street to find Fire Chief Randles moments after the tornado struck. The numbers of deaths would grow from that point on, and be posted at the EOC. Later, as the DMORT (Mortuary Science) effort helped to identify bodies, I would receive the listing of the names of the deceased. I remember saying a silent prayer with each new update, hoping it would be the last I would receive. As stated in earlier chapters, long after recovery efforts were effectively over, some who survived the storm succumbed to their injuries later in the hospital. It would be November before we would receive the final death toll: 161 confirmed tornado related deaths. At least we hoped it was the final number.

Twice a day, to and from work, I was reminded of the lives lost as I passed the location of the Mexican restaurant where I saw the victims in the minivan. For some reason, after the bodies were removed, the minivan remained in the parking lot for three months following May 22nd. Each time I drove by, I would glance in the direction of the vehicle and think about directing staff to have it removed. I finally concluded that perhaps the daily reminder was somehow important to keep me focused on the things that really matter.

In the days following the tornado, and as mentioned above, the fire department EOC personnel kept a running tally of those victims that were uncovered in the rubble. The number was listed on a whiteboard right next to a bank of radios where their personnel in the field called with updates. I would check this number at least three times a day for the first two weeks following the storm. The number was a real-time update and it created a problem for some of the different organizations working with us on disaster recovery. At a certain point, we would agree to use their number for updates in our press conferences and press releases. However, the coroner's office and the Highway Patrol were issuing their own numbers, which were not always consistent with our numbers given the time lapse and other challenges being faced in the identification process.

Late in the first week following the tornado, I was walking across the street to get to an afternoon press conference and a representative from the state's Department of Public Safety approached me asking me to change the terminology we were using in our releases from *bodies* to *human remains*. I was already late for the press conference and was extremely tired and frankly didn't fully comprehend what she was asking me to do just thirty seconds before I was on camera. I told her I wouldn't do it until I had time to think about it.

A couple of days later, Lane Roberts, Joplin's police chief, explained to me the challenges they were facing at the morgue and it made sense for the city to follow the coroner's lead. I agreed to use the term *human remains*, acknowledging difficulties involved at the morgue. Later, after the coroner had sufficient time and tests were conclusive, positive identity was established and we returned to reporting the number of deaths instead of the number of human remains.

Looking for Latina

Once the victims were identified, I received lists of the deceased in my office at the EOC. I would review the lists for people's names, to see if I recognized any of the victims. I also looked through the list to see if the lady I had lifted out of the church rubble along 20th Street was among the deceased. Even though the guy at the Community Dinner told me she was alive, I continued to scour the list looking for women the same age range as the woman I helped to lay in the grass at the north end of what was left of the Joplin Full Gospel Church. She had certainly appeared to be deceased, but none of the names and ages seemed to match the memory I had of the lady.

There had to be a reason why I couldn't find her name, I told myself. *Could she indeed be miraculously alive?* Fred Coombes, a man who was working along side me at the church on that first night supplied the name of the lady whom we assumed was dead after pulling her from the rubble: Latina Puebla. I met a woman later in October who also said she thought the lady's name was, Latina. Both verified that the woman I lifted from the heavy debris that night was very much alive. In fact, Fred had given me Latina Puebla's phone number. He said she worked for the post office in Carl Junction, Missouri, a small town a few miles north of Joplin.

On Tuesday, November 15th, I finally had things under control to the point that I decided to try and contact Latina. Even though I wanted to find out if, indeed, she had been the victim at the church, it was an odd phone call to make. Before I dialed the number, I remembered the painstaking work that night at the church and recalled the moment I lifted the lady out of the debris to gently set her down on the ground. It was the perception of all those working that area that the woman was clearly deceased; her body was lifeless and blue.

I called the number Fred gave me and let it ring a few times. The next sound I heard was a singing message from an answering machine: "I'm busy, I'm busy, I'm shockingly busy. I'd love to talk, but I can't, so leave a message." I was sort of paralyzed for a moment then realized this wasn't the kind of thing I could state on a message machine, so I hung up, determined to call her later in the day.

About an hour later, my administrative assistant, Vicki, called me and asked if I had called a lady named Latina. She was on the phone if I wanted to take her call. The next thing

I know, I was engaged in a phone conversation with the lady I thought had died in the church wreckage.

"Ms. Puebla, do you know who I am?" I asked first.

"Yes," I do," she softly answered.

"Do you also know I am the one who lifted you out of the church rubble on Sunday night, May 22nd?"

Again, she answered, "Yes, I know."

"Well, Ms. Puebla, I was so sure you had passed away. Is there a way you could stop by city hall for a few moments. I would love to meet you and…to tell you the truth, I need some closure."

Latina indicated Tuesday was her day off and she could drop by my office around 4:00 p.m. on that same afternoon.

I immediately called Mitch Randles and asked him to come over at 4:00 also, because I needed Mitch to help me validate whether or not this indeed was the woman pulled from the church. I had asked him a few days earlier if he would agree to meet her with me. I knew the circumstances were a little strange, but Mitch, being the kind of person he is, agreed willingly to be present at the meeting. At 3:45 p.m., my assistant, Sam, called me to tell me she had arrived. I asked him to see if Mitch was on his way. About five minutes before 4:00 p.m., I went upstairs to our second-floor conference room and peeked around the corner, like a little kid. I was suddenly so nervous.

There were two people sitting in the chairs, a man and a woman, but, I didn't see Mitch. I entered the room to greet them and introduced myself to an older man of about seventy-five in bib-overalls and a younger lady who introduced herself as Latina Puebla. The older gentleman was Latina's father. I would soon learn that he was also in the church on the night it blew apart.

I sat down across from them and asked to hear her story. She graciously obliged.

"My entire family was at the Joplin Full Gospel building that night for a Sunday evening service," Latina began. "My mother and father were there along with my sister; and my daughter was also there. We had just arrived and were talking to others about the hail from the approaching storm; waiting for the service to begin. Suddenly, the whole building collapsed around us. My entire family was trapped under the structure." Then Latina added, "I lost my sister and my daughter."

Not realizing she had experienced that kind of loss, I expressed my sincere condolences. By that time, Mitch had arrived and sat next to me while Latina continued, "I remember being pushed under the suffocating debris and trying to keep my sister talking, but I knew she was slipping away. I must have passed out. The next thing I recall was waking up in the grass and someone was pounding hard on my chest."

Later I would discover it was Fred Coombes girlfriend, Debbie Sturgis, who worked so hard to revive Latina that night. Debbie had recognized Latina as a friend and began to perform CPR on her. After a time, Debbie's efforts caused Latina to regurgitate, and then draw a long breath. Miraculously, she had been brought back to life.

Latina's parents had also been trapped and pulled from the remains of the church. Latina spoke of how she and her parents loaded their deceased loved ones in her father's battered van and drove to a nearby hospital in Carthage Missouri. I could only imagine the sadness in their hearts as they made that trip.

"Did you have any injuries from the experience at all?" I asked.

"No, I never even went to the doctor," Latina said, which I found amazing.

I asked later if she had cut her hair since the tornado, because I recalled the victim I pulled from the debris had long hair. "No," she answered, and then corrected herself. "Yes, yes, I have cut my hair since then."

Latina and her father told us many other stories about the church and its members regarding the storm. I hugged her as she turned to leave and thanked them both for coming by. I could tell Latina was appreciative for what I, and others, had done for her that terrible night.

After they left, I asked Mitch what he thought. He said, "Mark, have you thought about the possibility that it was her sister that you lifted out?" I'm sure I looked astonished at the prospect. I was so caught up in listening to Latina and her father's stories that such a thought never crossed my mind. Now there were more questions to ask. I went downstairs and decided to call Fred Coombes to see if he knew what Latina's sister looked like.

Fred happened to be with Debbie, his girlfriend, the one who had worked on bringing Latina back that night. "Well, I don't know for sure, but Debbie's here. She can tell you," he said, then passed the phone to Debbie.

"You know Latina's sister looked similar in size and appearance…," Debbie began, and then was interrupted when Fred took the phone again.

"Mark, you and Mitch had already left the church site by the time we got to Latina's daughter and sister," Fred offered.

Mitch and I didn't realize there was anyone else trapped in the rubble when we left the church to organize the overall recovery effort. That was also the reason we didn't recognize Latina's father from that night. He was still underneath the debris when we left.

It was settled. A miracle had occurred. The lady I pulled from the collapsed church was alive! Discovering Latina was alive due to our efforts and those of Debbie Sturgis, a friend who just wouldn't give up, is yet another example of "The Miracle of the Human Spirit."

The Miracles Continue

To date, some 110,000 registered volunteers have demonstrated "The Miracle of the Human Spirit" representing some 665,000 hours of volunteer work. They have selflessly set aside the demands of their own lives and have come to Joplin to help their fellow man in their time of need. The story of the Joplin tornado is not the powerful force of nature unleashed upon our city on that day in May. True, the storm ripped away and destroyed homes and personal possessions, but it did not destroy the values and beliefs of our citizens and volunteers. It did not destroy, but, in fact, revealed "The Miracle of the Human Spirit." Our challenge is to continue to invoke and direct that spirit into the rebuilding of our city and to live with it every day for the remainder of our lives. I challenge others to live the lessons learned in Joplin and to incorporate the value of life and the giving spirit that has taken place here into your lives; whether you are experiencing a tragedy or not.

Defining Moment of our Lives

> "Everybody's going to know people who are dead. You could have probably dropped a nuclear bomb on the town and I don't think it would have done near as much damage as it did."
>
> —Zach Tusinger, CNN iReporter

- 5:17 p.m. (CST) on May 22nd, 2011, a super cell thunderstorm moved from southeast Kansas to Missouri. The National Weather Service issued a tornado warning and personnel at Joplin's 911 Center activated the city's sirens reflecting the tornado warning in three-minute blasts of sound.

- 5:24 p.m. a multi-vortex tornado quickly formed on the city of Joplin's western border at a location adjacent to a new fire station that was under construction. It proceeded in a northeasterly direction and picked up in speed and intensity as it roared through the city.

- 5:37 p.m. the sirens were sounded in Joplin a second time by city personnel.

- 5:41 p.m. the tornado strikes the Cedar Ridge subdivision on the city's west end, destroying homes in its path. Moments later, the Sunset Ridge subdivision is struck as the tornado made its way to 26th Street and Maiden Lane where it is thought to have gained strength to become a storm categorized with EF5 force winds. St. John's Hospital and Cunningham Park were devastated in its wake.

- 5:45 p.m. The tornado continued its path through residential neighborhoods, where it hit the city's main commercial area on Rangeline Road. After leaving Joplin, it ripped through the tiny city of Duquesne and destroyed more residences there, then lessened in intensity and crossed I-44 and continued into the countryside before dying out.

Storm Facts

- The tornado that shredded a good portion of Joplin was 22.1 miles long and a half to three quarters of a mile wide at its peak with six of those miles spanning from the west border to the eastern border of our city.

- The Enhanced Fujita scale for measuring wind speed rated it an EF5, because the wind speed with the tornado was in excess of 200 miles per hour.

- One hundred and sixty-one citizens would lose their lives as a result of the tornado with well over a thousand injuries.

- Over 7,500 homes were impacted by the storm, with 3,500 of those structures either being rendered uninhabitable or destroyed.

- Approximately 500 businesses were impacted with many of those being wiped out completely.

- An estimated 18,000 cars were totaled or damaged.

- A third of our town was essentially gone.

- The Joplin tornado was the deadliest tornado in the United States since the National Weather Service began keeping official records in 1950. In terms of lost lives, the Joplin tornado was the worst in the United States since 181 lives were lost in a tornado in Woodward, Oklahoma in 1947 and the seventh worst in the history of our country.

- Eighty percent of tornadoes in the United States are of the EF0 or EF1 variety. Less than 1 percent of tornadoes are an EF4 or stronger.

- The average width of a tornado is 500 feet across with an average length of five miles. The Joplin tornado was anywhere from one-half to three-quarters of a mile wide.

- The Joplin tornado left behind 3 million cubic yards of debris.

- There was not much that was typical about the massive storm except to point out that most tornadoes occur in late afternoon, and in this one respect, the Joplin tornado was typical.

Personal Perspective

Before May 22nd, the tornados I had seen appeared to swoop down to the ground, and then lift off momentarily, only to touch down again somewhere further along its path. The Joplin tornado seemed to stay on the ground for its entire route through one of Joplin's most densely populated areas.

Looking back at videos of the tornado, it appeared as a very big, black funnel moving through Joplin. Tornado funnels are actually accumulated water vapor, combined with a tremendous force of wind, but appear dark in color due to the large amount of debris sucked up into the vortex.

The amount of debris that the storm left was indescribable. I had directed city staff to shoot video of the storm field the day after the tornado. I thought it would be important to have this footage to demonstrate the sheer and utter wreckage. As mentioned before, to a person, everyone who saw the carnage in the aftermath said that pictures and news accounts didn't do the damage justice. It was as if the camera lens and the written word were inadequate vehicles by which to describe the magnitude of the storm and the resultant damage. It was a little frustrating for me to attempt to describe the debris and the extent of the destruction to friends and relatives visiting the area after the debris was removed. At some point, we may release the videos to be able to tell the entire story of the storm.

I was not in the tornado. I was at my home in the southern section of Joplin, but looking back on it, I was aware of the eerie calm and quiet before and after the storm. This effect might have been the result of the vacuum created by the storm istelf. I was also amazed at the pinkish hue to the sky after the storm.

Different things stand out in people's minds as a result of the tornado. I mentioned earlier in the book, the loss of so many manhole lids in the storm area. That is very odd. Any kid who has ever messed around and tried to lift a manhole cover knows how incredibly heavy they are. They are also flush to the ground and generally are lifted with a crowbar-type tool by a guy who performs physical tasks for a living. It stretches my imagination to think of the force of nature that could pick up a manhole lid, then cause it to disappear.

When I asked the National Weather Service team that was in Joplin after the tornado to perform an after-incident audit in regard to how strong the winds were, I was told they hadn't performed the calculation yet, but they mentioned the parking blocks in the parking lot of St. John's Regional Hospital. Most striking to them was how these 300-pound curbs that were fastened to the ground flew 90 feet into the air.

To provide another level of perspective on the storm debris in Joplin, Joplin officials spoke to a representative of Phillips and Jordan, who worked both the cleanup of debris from the World Trade Center and who performed the initial work in Joplin. The estimate from Phillips and Jordan on that incredible effort at the World Trade Center was 2 million cubic yards. The estimate for debris removal in Joplin was 3 million cubic yards.

On November 4, 2011, the Weather Channel's Dr. Greg Forbes, a severe weather expert, issued a report saying the estimated 2.8 billion dollars in damage makes Joplin the costliest tornado ever. Dr. Forbes apparently began his career as a graduate student alongside Ted Fujita who created the intensity scale for tornadoes. He called Joplin's tornado one of the "Superoutbreak 2011" tornados along with the April tornados in Tuscaloosa and Hackleberg, Alabama. The second costliest according to his analysis which was adjusted for inflation was an 1896 tornado in St. Louis, Missouri, at $2.55 billion and the third costliest was the 2011 Tuscaloosa tornado, 2.2 billion dollars. Dr. Forbes adds that the "superoutbreak" term is being used in this instance for only the second time. The first time was April, 1973 in Xenia, Ohio, about an hour from where I grew up, which claimed 34 lives.

Dr. Forbes continued his analysis with his admittedly subjective attempt to combine deaths and damage to rank Joplin's 2011 tornado as the third worst ever behind the famous 1925 Tri-State tornado and the 1896 St. Louis tornado.

It Could Have Been Much Worse

What amazes most people that I have talked to is that we only had 161 deaths. Joplin High School had just graduated some 450 seniors at the Leggett and Platt Center at Missouri Southern University only moments before the tornado. Had the ceremony been held at Joplin High School or if the storm had occurred during the week while school was in session or as the estimated 270,000 a day that travel daily to Joplin were in town, there is no telling how high the fatality count would be.

Despite the day of the week and the time of the tornado, it is still hard to believe that more people weren't lost given the path of the storm. There is no doubt in my mind that sounding the siren a second time saved lives. The National Weather Service performed a study released in July of 2011 saying many Joplin residents ignored the first siren but many reacted to the second which sounded four minutes before the tornado struck. Another important factor to consider is that warning sirens are not intended to alert people indoors. They are intended for outdoor notification and if one hears it indoors it is by chance, not design. Accordingly, the sirens did work, as according to the National Weather Service July 2011 report, only 14 percent of the deaths from the storm came from those in vehicles and outdoors.

Every Joplin resident has a story to tell about May 22nd. They can recall exactly where they were, how they felt, and what they saw in the moments during and after. Locally, it's like the common question asked after every national tragedy… "Where were you when you heard that John F. Kennedy had been assassinated?" "Where you when the Twin Towers fell on September 11th in New York City?" Hardly a day goes by that I don't hear another story or the conversation doesn't turn to, "Where were you during the tornado?"

Sure, all of us felt utterly helpless in the face of such a destructive force, but we felt something else, too; something well worth remembering. Heroes were born in those terrifying moments, bravery was demonstrated in the most profound ways, and we witnessed so many acts of kindness that our faith in mankind was restored. Faith was deepened, and hope and dependence on God was never more evident.

At the moment of silence ceremony we had a week after the storm, I told the people of Joplin that 5:41 p.m. on May 22, 2011, would be the defining moment in our lives. Now, nearly a year later, I believe it more than ever. And, I am proud to say, Joplin has chosen to define itself, not by the tragedy of the tornado, but rather in the manner in which we responded to what happened to us on May 22nd, 2011.

Special Thanks

I want to thank Tate Publishing & Enterprises and especially Creative Project Director, Rita Tate for assisting me in preparing the manuscript for publishing. I appreciated Rita's counsel and encouragement every step along the way. Also, thanks to my wife, Lois, for transcribing notes and organizing the material and being a listening ear and constant source of help with the many details to be covered.

—Mark Rohr, Spring, 2012

Those Who Lost Their Lives Due to Joplin Tornado May 22, 2011

- Jose Olimpo Alvarez

- Maria de Lourdes Alvarez-Torres

- Barbara Ann Morgan Anderson

- Sarah Lee Sherfy Anderson

- William Austin Anderson

- Grace L. Aquino

- Dale Lawrence Arsenault

- Cyrus Edward Ash, Jr

- Bruce Baillie

- Robert W. Baker

- Robert Eugene Bateson

- Dorthey Lee Calvert Bell

- Regina Mae Bloxham

- Barbara Fuller Boyd

- Lathe E. Bradfield
- Burnice M. Bresee
- Ramona Mae Peavey Bridgeford
- Leo Earl Brown
- Hugh Odell Buttram
- Tami Leigh Campbell
- Arriyinnah Savannah Carmona
- Moises Carmona
- Shante Marie Caton
- Trentan Maurice Steven Caton
- Rev. Raymond LeRoy Chew, Sr
- Clyde L. Coleman
- Carolane Jean Burton Collins
- Lois Ada McKinney Comfort
- Keenan Krice Conger
- James Van Cookerly
- Edmond Andrew Cooper
- Vicki Lynn Cooper
- Alice L. Cope
- Teddy Ray Copher
- Malisa Ann Crossley

- Adam Dewayne Darnaby
- Patricia Elaine Dawson
- Michael Wayne Dennis
- Nancy Elizabeth Thornberry Douthitt
- Ellen Jeanette Doyle
- Faith Constance Dunn
- Amonda Sue Eastwood-Pryor
- Richard Allen Elmore
- Randy Edward England
- Mark Lewis Farmer
- Ida Mildred Finley
- Betty Jo Burlington Fisher
- Robert S. Fitzgerald
- Rick E. Fox
- Marsha Ann Winkler Frost
- Sebastian C. Frost
- Charles Kenneth Gaudsmith
- Billie Jo Gideon
- Robert M. Griffin
- Steven Joseph Haack-Stephens
- Paul Eugene Haddock

- Johnna Jean Stanbery Hale
- Leola M. Hardin
- Caley Lantz Hare
- Dorothy Viola Gray Hartman
- Dee Ann Kelly Hayward
- Judy Rae Bryan Head
- Glenn Wayne Holland
- Lorie Marie Lippoldt Holland
- Ronnie D. Hollaway
- Charlotte "Char" Hopwood
- Harli Jayce Howard
- Hayze Cole Howard
- Russell Thomas Howard
- Iona Lee Hull
- Wendy Ann Wasson Istas
- Jane E. Jaynes
- Melisa Renee Johnson
- Dorothy M. Johnston
- Cheryl Lynne Jones
- Kathy Susan Keling
- James David Kendrick

- Abraham "Abe" H. Khoury
- Stanley D. Kirk
- Geneva Eutsler Koler
- Tedra J. Kuhn
- Donald Wayne Lansaw, Jr
- Bruce A. Lievens
- Billie Sue Huff Little
- Skyuler Ignatius Logsdon
- Christopher Don Lucas
- Patricia Anne Mann
- Rachel Kristine Markham
- Nancy Ann Grinage Martin
- Janice Kay Yeager McKee
- Jesse Len McKee
- James Edward McKeel
- Mary Lois McKeel
- LaDonna S. Journot McPurdy
- Randall Elvin Mell
- Angelina Ann Menapace
- Doris Marie Finley Menhusen-Montgomery
- Ronald Dale Meyer

- Lorna "Kay" Wildrix Miller
- Ray Donald "Tripp" Miller, III
- Suzanne M. Francione Mock
- Edith "Edie" Louise Froelich Moore
- Esterlita M. Moore
- Sally Ann Harris Moulton
- G. Nadine Morris Mulkey
- Edmund Vincent Mullaney
- Sharyl Anyssa San Miguel Nelsen
- William Richard Norton
- Dennis Melvin Osborn
- Charles E Oster
- Shirley Ann Parker
- Nichole Pearish
- Mary Joyce Thurman Perry
- James Benjamin John Peterson
- Anna Pettek
- Jay Petty, Jr
- Hallie Marie Agleton Piquard
- Natalia Marie Puebla
- Troy Douglas Ramey

- Shelly Marie Gray Ramsey
- Loretta L. Randall
- Cheryl E. Spruce Rantz
- Darlene Kay Hall Ray
- Virgil Thomas Reid
- Johnnie Ray Richey
- Vicki P. Robertson
- Cayla Ann Selsor Robinson
- Keith Derek Robinson
- Margaret Ellen Row
- Virginia Mae Templeton Salmon
- Grace Marie Dummit Sanders
- Thomas B. Sarino
- Tonja Lee Sawyer
- Frances Ann Worm Scates
- Gladys Juanita Stanton Seay
- Daniel Wayne Shirley
- Judy Lee Brown Smith
- Luther Gene Smith
- Nicholaus Adam Smith
- Shyrell Lee Cranor Smith

- Lois Laverne Schnook Sparks
- Betty J. Toops Stogsdill
- Ralph Gilbert Stover
- JT Strickland
- Gregan Douglas Sweet
- Jefferson Taylor
- Kayleigh Savannah Teal
- Heather Leigh Terry
- Sandra Kay Thomas
- John L. Thomas, Jr
- Zachary Delbert Treadwell
- Margaret Ann Unger Tutt
- Michael E. "Mikey" Tyndall
- Darian Darlene Vanderhoofven
- Joshua Dean Vanderhoofven
- Miguel "Mikey" Vasquez-Castillo
- Miles Dean Wells
- Tiera Nicole Whitley
- Douglas Earl Williams
- Zachary "Zach" Allen Williams
- Charles William Writer

Map of Tornado's Path Through Joplin, May 22nd, 2011

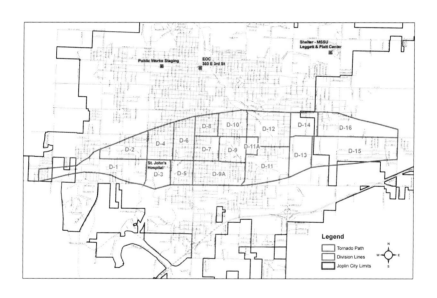

Speech Delivered on November 22, 2011

Mark Rohr, City Manager, Joplin, MO
(Six month anniversary of Joplin Tornado)

I want to personally thank everyone for coming out here today to be participants in this very important moment in the city's history. We gather here today to pay tribute to those that we have lost as a result of the May 22nd tornado. We gather here today to thank the many that have come to Joplin to help our town and we gather here today to look towards Joplin's future.

I asked you, on May 29th, to honor those that we had lost by channeling our feelings and emotions for the departed into our overall recovery efforts. You, the citizens of Joplin, have done so in ways and to extremes that I never dreamed of at the moment of silence observation held that day. Joplin stands as a shining example to our state, country and to the world of what the time-honored American virtues of compassion, hard work and dogged determination can accomplish.

Today, we dedicate the first of 161 trees in Cunningham Park that will serve as the living embodiment of the spirits of those that we have lost. These trees will be nurtured by our tender hands and those of our children and our children's chil-

dren, in this hallowed ground. They will transcend the tempo-
ral limitations of those of us in attendance here today, as a living
reminder of those no longer with us. I daresay that these trees
will be amongst the most well-kept in the state of Missouri.

To the 113,000 registered volunteers that have come to
Joplin's aid, mere words and actions expressing thanks are
inadequate in acknowledging your efforts. You have reaf-
firmed my faith in mankind but more importantly you have
demonstrated to the world what can be accomplished by setting aside egos, agendas and the demands of your own lives
to help your fellow man. It is a lesson in life that we all need
to remember and we all need to live long after the fog of
the emergency and its aftermath have lifted. You, the volunteers, are the living embodiment of "The Miracle of the
Human Spirit." In a humble attempt to express our gratitude,
we have created a memorial (to our northeast) that reflects
in concentric circles the four stages of our disaster recovery, along with a metal band representing the Miracle of the
Human Spirit wristband. At the center of the memorial, we
would like to have a bronze sculpture with figures representing the volunteers and actual debris from the storm cast in
bronze. This debris will serve as a touchstone for both you
and your succeeding generations to come to return to Joplin
to commemorate your experience in this very special human
movement. In the same manner that you helped Joplin, your
offspring can demonstrate their participation in this unique
effort by simulating their assistance in lifting the debris in
the sculpture.

We are also blessed here today to dedicate two distinct
water features in Cunningham Park. The use of water is

intended to demonstrate the growth and regenerative properties of that element. For what really do we all have but this moment in time amongst our friends and relatives and our hopes for a bright and verdant tomorrow? The tornado can take away that which we own but it can't strip away our values, beliefs and our hopes for a better future.

On that fateful day in May, nature let loose a powerful force that cleaved our city in two and rendered unspeakable damage. But in doing so, it unleashed an even more powerful force much stronger than the winds that day. It is a force that has drawn this town together and has united us in a common effort that will make Joplin better than it was before. We are forever linked by our common experiences on that very uncommon day. We are brothers and sisters of the storm. We are survivors, that will not be defined by the tornado but rather by the manner in which we responded to circumstances thrust upon us. And in that spirit, I say to those Joplinites that have sought refuge elsewhere-You may have been welcomed in your new circumstances but those that surround you can never fully identify with what happened to you, like all of us here can and I bid to you here today Come home to Joplin, Come home to Joplin, Come home to Joplin.

Song Dedicated to the City of Joplin

Sing Again

Copyright, 2010 by Mark Laperle

I wish I could take away the pain,
A broken heart can bring; it changes everything.
I'd gladly give you sunshine for the rain,
Then by the grace of God, your heart would sing again.

I can't know the burden that you bear,
Winter snows and then weeping willows bend.
But I know your sorrow is meant to share,
And by the grace of God, your heart will sing again.

In the darkest hour of your deepest, darkest night,
Know the dawn is coming and you're gonna be alright!

When the sunlight paints the morning sky,
And you remember when, hope's eternal Friend,
Will kiss away each teardrop from your eyes.
Then by the grace of God, your heart will sing again.

The Ten Tenets of Disaster Management

Mark Rohr

1. Get Organized

2. Understand There will be Trial and Error

3. Find a Way for Everyone to Participate Either by Donating or Volunteering

4. Don't Get Seduced by the Limelight—Stay focused on What is Important

5. Stay Directly Connected to the Area and People Impacted by the Disaster

6. Designate *One* Spokesperson to update progress and Reassure the Public Regarding the Future

7. Local Leadership is the Essential Ingredient

8. Be Aware of the Psychological Mood of the Community

9. Use the Attention Created by the Event to Benefit the Community. Don't be Overwhelmed or Victimized by it.

10. Limit the number of People Given Access to the Actual Operation Center

Other Information

For more information about volunteering or donating to
the Joplin recovery effort see: www. Rebuildjoplin.com

To order additional copies of
JOPLIN: The Miracle of the Human Spirit

www.tatepublishing.com
1-888-361-9473

Proceeds from this book will be directed
toward disaster recovery efforts